NOT 1

MORE DAY!

Rise above your circumstances and live.

Jacq 'Mizjaq' Green

NOT 1 MORE DAY

Copyright © 2019 by KoLKoB Publishing

All rights reserved. No part of this book may be reproduced or transmitted in any form or by any means without written permission from the author.

ISBN (978-1-7335822-0-9)

Printed in USA by HTM3 Solutions

<u>**Dedication**</u>

"That we should be to the praise of His glory." Believers are either in their lives to be "living epistles of Christ, to be known and read of all men," as instances of the power of Divine grace, or they are to set forth His praises by ascribing everything to His grace and nothing to their own merit. - T.C.

<u>**About the Author**</u>

Jacq-Johnese, most affectionally referred to as Mizjaq, uses inspiring, insightful and interactive presentations to communicate life-changing concepts to audiences of all ages. As an author, Certified Vision Board and Life Coach, she is a profound linguistic activist with much respect and appreciation for the power of words and their impact on the quality of everyday life experiences.

Even as a child, this native Houstonian was greatly disturbed by the noticeable disparity amongst various races, socio-economic groups and genders. Often, she would question her parents about why certain groups of people dominated specific areas, and why there were so many living in poverty while others lived in abundance. Her acute social awareness, curiosity and discomfort were heightened further when she attended Prairie View A&M University, worked for a Fortune 500 software company and later taught in both private & public schools. Clearly, the playing fields were unequal… inequity ruled.

It wasn't until she read in the Bible that God was no respecter of persons – that she understood the concept of wanting everyone to benefit from the good things in life, regardless of what they looked like or where they were from.

It is with great fervor and faith today that she coaches, counsels and encourages others to get past the past, overcome barriers to success and boldly press towards a brighter tomorrow. Her most recent work, "**NOT 1 MORE DAY**!" embodies Mizjaq's purpose - which is to provide others with a voice that will empower them to realize, activate and exercise their God-given right to an abundant life. (**John 10:10**)

Her motto is, "You must articulate to accelerate by speaking in agreement with God's word; then trust Him to lead you into purpose and manifest your heart's desires!"

In obedience to **Habakkuk 2:2** - Her vision has been written for your closer walk with Him!

<u>Foreward</u>

"Teaching is by example," Albert Schweitzer shared with us. Jesus taught his disciples by example. That was his primary means of messaging. To this day, it remains the best method of transforming others.

Our writer humbles herself by offering examples, thru confessions, of her own shortfalls. Her story stimulates a bond with the reader, walking hand-in-hand on the journey towards **NOT 1 MORE DAY**. This experience is like finding that long lost best friend. It is a journey with a disciple, first passing a time of reflection and imagination, then transitioning into a person-to-person communication with God, followed by a meeting with the Holy Spirit, an event, which must be experienced. The result will be a renewal and a transformation of character, which will become known, when inwardly experienced.

A legendary entertainer was scraped from the lowly streets of New York as a lad and granted the opportunity to attend summer camp. After several days, the young camper expressed to his bunkmate "this is the first time I've had three meals a day, clean sheets, and nice people all about." He wondered aloud, "How did this happen?" His bunkmate answered, "Because someone cared." Before drifting off to sleep, the youngster prayed, thanking God for "Someone."

Your "long lost best friend," and that "someone," is Mizjaq Green. She brushes all the sharp pebbles to the side, and believes in you, all the way. May God Bless you both, as you blaze this path to a brighter day together.

Frank H. Mayfield, Jr.
The Literary Club of Cincinnati (1980 – Present)

<u>**Introduction**</u>

"Your talent is God's gift to you. What you do with it is your gift back to God." **Leo Buscaglia**

Each day that God gives you breath and allows you to open your eyes is a gift! What you decide to do with that gift is totally up to you. The very moment you acknowledge and embrace this truth … you will experience both a sense of appreciation and accountability to activate the freedom and power to change your reality. My purpose for writing this book is to partner with you along your journey towards a deeper spiritual connection with your Creator. In so doing, self-empowerment, self-actualization and dream realization will result.

The words on these pages will awaken your awareness of God's presence in your everyday musings of life, His ability to navigate you through and to the blessings He has reserved in your name if you simply ask, and His unconditional love and favor towards you.

Using an amalgamation of life lessons, God's written word and those of others, to make known the many signposts, which until today, may have been hidden from your sight, I welcome you to experience my walking and talking with Him. These subtle indicators, once recognized in the stories and accounts shared within these pages, are sure to inspire you to fortify your spiritual relationships, unleash your authority, fill you with a surplus of courage to create the life you truly deserve, and guide you along the path to achieve your heart's desire.

If where you are right now (spiritually, physically, relationally, financially, professionally or emotionally) is not where you long to be, you have purchased the right book at the right time. Your wait is over: the hour has come. I stand in agreement with you and declare in the mighty Name of Jesus that **NOT 1 MORE DAY** will you be confused, anxious, stressed or depressed about who you are, whose you are or who you are destined to become. And so, it begins …

"An Affirming Pledge to Myself"

This day has been given to me fresh and clear.

I can either use it or throw it away.

I promise myself that I shall use this day to its fullest

realizing it can never come back again.

I realize this is my life to use or to throw away.

I am the only person

who has the power to decide what I will be;

I make myself what I am."

Marva Collins

CHAPTER 1

The Gift is Present Within

You are God's gift to the world, and each day you're alive is His gift to you. He had a specific plan and purpose in mind for your creation and no one can be better you than you!

In fact, the exact timing, location and circumstances present when you were born were Divinely orchestrated. So, in case you didn't know just how special you are or how purpose-filled your presence here on earth is, don't worry, you won't have to wonder **NOT 1 MORE DAY**!

The song, 'This Little Light of Mine' brings back such joyful and happy feelings for me. Oh, wouldn't it be wonderful if we could experience that childlike innocence and bliss in the midst of toxic family relationships, a stressful workplace, a broken spirit or financial difficulty?

To determine in the heart and mind that no matter what, "I'm gonna let my light shine!" To not let the devil, other people's opinions of me, the medical report, my past failures or disappointments snuff it out. To possess the strength to rise above unpleasant situations and circumstances, boldly declaring the power of your light by saying, "My God gave it to me, and I'm gonna let it shine!" Well, guess what?

He did give 'light' to you, and you can let it 'shine' because you were born to 'shine'.

Say 2 Self: *The 'light' within me is meant to shine brightly amidst the darkness in my world.*

You have something uniquely yours that others need to see. Something that radiates from the inside of you and has the power to illuminate, inspire and positively impact the lives of others. Something that the enemy desperately wants to keep suppressed and out of sight … he hates it when you 'shine.' Why?

Simply because darkness thrives in darkness, and your 'shining light' represents your Heavenly Father, your **TAGs** (Talents/Abilities/Gifts) – an exceptional brilliance which is certain to bring 'light' (consciousness) to others.

Accordingly, **Matthew 5:16** commands you to *"Let your light so shine before men, that they may see your good works, and glorify your Father which is in Heaven."* Your 'shining light' signifies adoration and appreciation to God; a presentation to the universe of the gift of life He's bestowed. You were created to let your light shine, and I am honored to be one of the vessels He's chosen to show you how to tap into your purpose and get your 'shine' on!

> **Say 2 Self:** My purpose here on earth is linked to my light.

The problems you seem to solve so effortlessly for others, the innovative business ideas you always have, or the way your words naturally flow when you present information … that's your light. It could also simply be your contagious smile and joyful demeanor, so keep shining!

As an only child I loved to play 'preach' to my dolls and stuffed animals. In fact, I would conduct the entire church service from beginning to end. I prayed over them, played the toy piano while singing to them, collected a pretend offering, read the scripture of the day and then delivered a hooping sermon which concluded with an invitation to discipleship.

Of course, I had my essential tools of the trade: a face cloth to catch my sweat and wipe the corners of my mouth like I'd seen older Baptist preachers do, two lit candles on each side of my open Bible (both parents smoked so matches were plentiful) ☐, a sand bucket for tithes/offering collections and a glass of water or orange juice to sip on between my preaching hoops. When I tired of preaching, I would go outside to the garage where my chalkboard was nailed to the wall and play 'teach'.

My classroom consisted of my most faithful 'church members' - dolls and stuffed animals - who never missed a lesson. Attentively they sat at a small burnt orange Samsonite table with white legs, accompanied by four matching chairs. But on days when I was feeling more entrepreneurial, I'd set up my home office in our den (family room), where I had a toy cash register, lots of pens/paper, a ring of old keys, my daddy's outdated business account check registers and an unplugged rotary dial telephone I used to receive my customer's calls.

For many years, my mother kept the 'check' I wrote her, in the amount of one million dollars, from my lucrative home business, ministry and teaching. She later told me that I'd spelled the word million correctly and that the zeros accurately matched the written number. My most generous gift tickled her tremendously. Not bad for a seven-year-old, right?

Now some may think, "She was just a kid playing, so what's the big deal?" Well, as I grew up those play professions became the very threads woven intricately into the colorful quilting of my adult life. In my teens I joined the choir in high school and at church, entered various impromptu speaking competitions, and played a real home piano/organ. Additionally, my affinity for the written word caused me to journal and compose poems as a hobbies.

At twenty-six, I began working in ministry which included conducting in-home Bible studies, leading women's prayer group meetings, teaching Sunday school and speaking at area churches on numerous occasions. Professionally, I facilitated corporate training globally and wouldn't you know it … ended up teaching in both public/private institutions of education for students from all walks of life ranging from ages four to seventy-three.

That's right, my oldest student was Ms. Gladys, a precious grandmother of five and GED candidate who was as serious about getting her diploma. At the time of this writing, I've yet to write my mother a real million-dollar check, but I do believe it is coming!

Just as I had done as a child, as an adult, I found myself jumping back and forth from teaching, training and ministering to others in an attempt to use my 'light' and let it 'shine'. Although I lacked the full awareness of my **TAGs** (Talents/Abilities/Gifts), clarity of purpose and a committed vision, in retrospect I was on a noticeable path. However, not having a solid awareness of my **TAGs** delayed my evolution from existing to living. Undeniably those varied experiences, coupled with knowledge gained therein laid the foundation for all that I am today. You see, even though I played preaching, teaching and entrepreneuring, I couldn't seem to really focus on one area or blend them into the consciousness of my 'light'.

As a result, I ended up wasting a tremendous amount of time and shine along the way. Or so I thought. You see, God's word promises us that ALL things work together for the good for those who love the Lord and are called according to His purpose. **Romans 8:28**

The point of this short trip down memory lane, other than to provoke a chuckle or two, is to enlighten you to how even as children, our **TAGs** (Talents/Abilities/Gifts) are present. God allows us to playfully gravitate towards our 'light' in childlike innocence.

Pause here and take a moment to recall how you played as a child. Think about your interests and personality. Reflect upon what you enjoyed doing and which tasks were easiest or what activities most excited you. Compare these things to the work you are doing now. How similar are they? How different are they? Are you surprised?

For some, your light was innately known, and you boldly communicated it to others. Somehow, you already knew you wanted to be a law enforcer, doctor, beautician, politician, model, artist, etc., at an early age, and when asked, you confidently responded. Maybe you were fortunate enough to have parents who recognized your giftedness and helped guide you along the path.

For others, you may not have had a clue about your light or your **TAGs** (Talents/Abilities/Gifts), but someone along the way (like a teacher, friend or relative) spoke indelible words of encouragement pointing you towards your 'light'. Perhaps even until this very moment you were unsure about God's purpose for your life, or a bit unclear about your **TAGs** (Talents/Abilities/Gifts).

My hope is that while you read these words you sit and bask in the brink of knowing. Whatever thoughts drift or surface in your mind as you think back … consider them.

Try to recall any recurring habits, hobbies or interests; these are areas of **TAG** possibility. If there is a particular activity, or skill coming to mind, continue to pay attention to **that** inkling inside and tap into **that**.

Cultivate **that**.

Pray about **that**.

I challenge you to decide, today, to pursue **that** without fear; it could very well be your **TAG**.

Work to develop **that** with all confidence and Godly assurance … you were made for this! Decree, declare and determine to waste **NOT 1 MORE DAY** dedicated to the darkness of a disconnected dead-end job; **NOT 1 MORE DAY** pining away in the pit of passionless pursuits; **NOT 1 MORE DAY** living lifelessly from the lull of a lukewarm relationship; **NOT 1 MORE DAY** being held hostage in the hollow hopeless hole of a helpless state of mind.

You were created in His image … the Greater One lives in you and longs to use you as His vessel here on Earth. He has amazing plans for you, and as you hold this book in your hands, He will begin speaking His purpose to your heart. Listen. In the words of one of my favorite authors, life coaches and motivational speakers, Anthony Robbins, it's time to awaken the giant within!

(SSI) Soul Self Inventory:

1. Am I ready to let my 'light' shine? Why? Why not?
2. What will it take for my 'light' to begin to shine?
3. Is there a 'light' I've seen shining in others that also flickers in me?
4. What are my **TAGs**?
5. Who has said something to me that confirms what I believe my **TAGs** are?

<u>Prayer 2 Pray Today:</u>

Heavenly Father,

I believe you created me for a specific purpose and have equipped me with everything I need to fulfill your perfect will for my life. I acknowledge the light you've given me, and I thank you for choosing me. Thank you for showing me glimpses of your plan and giving me a dream (a burning desire) deep down in my spirit to make a difference in this world. Thank you, Lord God, for patiently waiting for me to arrive at this point of readiness and for bringing me into full awareness. Thank you for my journey thus far and for giving me a bright new beginning.

Now Lord, in your Son Jesus' name, I ask you to give me the wisdom, courage and Divine connections necessary to bring my light into complete fruition. I invite you to use me as your vessel, your mouthpiece and your hands extended for those you have assigned to me as they witness and are transformed by my shine. Please continue to lead me and guide me in the way that you see fit to prepare me for your service, and I declare that with your help, I will waste **NOT 1 MORE DAY** *of my giftedness due to fear or distractions from the busyness of this life. Now Father God, I place my total trust in you knowing and believing that with you ALL things are possible.*

Amen.

Chapter 2:

Identify Who & Whose You Are

> "Then, with the eyes of your hearts enlightened, you will know the confidence that is produced by God having called you, the rich glory that is his inheritance among the saints."
> **Ephesians 1:18**

You MUST know and understand who you are! I repeat, you MUST know and understand who you are! The Bible warns us in **Hosea 4:6** that God's people are destroyed for lack of knowledge, and He wants you to know your real identity, your due inheritance and your true importance. This knowing is the lifeblood of everything connected to you in this life. Knowing who you are, understanding whose you are and recognizing what does/does not belong to you has the power to make or break you.

On the contrary, your adversary, those used by him and the world system in which we operate know exactly who you are, what you are capable of and how big of an impact God created you to make on the rest of us.

Accordingly, many strange and familiar foes alike, seek to prey on and benefit from your lack of true self-awareness. They are identity thieves who work overtime to destroy your confidence, dim your shine and kill your desires to dream or live an abundant life. Their devices are designed to keep you down and bound - wallowing in a sea of misery, misfortune and mundane mediocrity with them. But of course, I have some exciting news for you … your **SDTs** (self-defeating thoughts), disappointing outcomes and doubt ridden days end today!

NOT 1 MORE DAY will you wake up believing that you were a mistake, that your life doesn't matter or that you are just here to get a job, pay bills, grow old and die. You *are* somebody, somebody fearfully and wonderfully made to live here in this season for a specific reason.

Someone, somewhere, is waiting on you to take your place on the stage of life, to speak up and speak out, and to allow your light to lead their way out of darkness. But first, you MUST know that you know who and whose you are.

This self-knowing brings to mind a poem I taught to my Pre-K 4 students many years ago written by the late Countee Cullen. His resounding message continues to serve in this 21st Century as a powerful awakening tool for all regardless of age, race, geographic location and socio-economic background. In **<u>Hey Black Child</u>**, you will find a rhetorical stirring of the vast potential lying within as Countee poses a series of deep soul-searching questions like:

> *"Do you know who you are ...*
>
> *who you really are?"*
>
> *"Do you know you are strong ...*
>
> *I mean, really strong?"*

<u>**Your True Identity**</u>

> *"Behold what manner of love the Father has bestowed on us, that we should be called children of God! Therefore, the world does not know us, because it did not know Him."*
> **1 John 3:1**

Hey God's Child, you have been lied to. NO, you are NOT a mistake or a misfit. NO, you are NOT just like your sister, brother, mother or father. NO, you are NOT a loser or a failure. NO, you are NOT a has-been or a wanna-be. No, you are NOT defined by your job title. NO, you are NOT qualified by your degree or diploma, attractive because of your dress size, granted acceptance by your zodiac sign, fraternity or sorority name. NO, you are NOT to be validated by your relationship status, your financial portfolio, your credit score, your address. NO, you are not your sexual preference or doomed by your past. You are NOT too late. You are NOT too young. You are NOT too old.

And No … you are NOT alone!

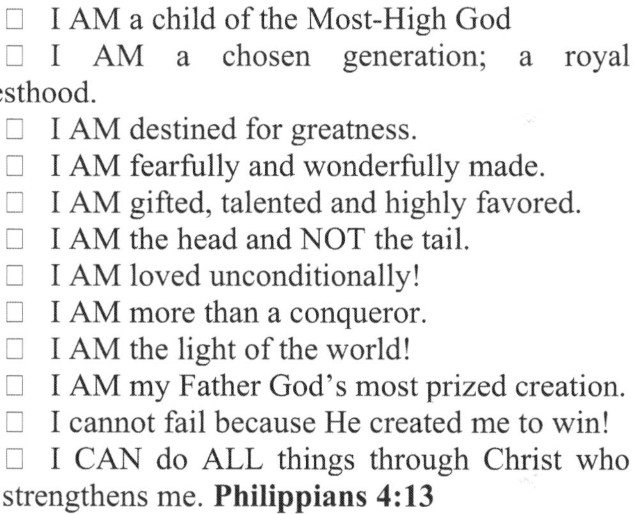

- I AM a child of the Most-High God
- I AM a chosen generation; a royal priesthood.
- I AM destined for greatness.
- I AM fearfully and wonderfully made.
- I AM gifted, talented and highly favored.
- I AM the head and NOT the tail.
- I AM loved unconditionally!
- I AM more than a conqueror.
- I AM the light of the world!
- I AM my Father God's most prized creation.
- I cannot fail because He created me to win!
- I CAN do ALL things through Christ who strengthens me. **Philippians 4:13**

Now, imagine with me for a moment if you had known who you really were 5, 10, 20 or perhaps even 30 years ago. How different would your life be? Faith in God be? Personal relationships be? Finances be? Career be?

With all those wonderfully amazing possibilities and revelations dangling around in your mind, let's move full speed ahead with what you DO know at this moment! Take what you have envisioned, all that's been awakened and commit to making that become your present reality.

Every single time you look in the mirror or catch a glimpse of yourself, make a concerted effort to remind yourself who you ARE. From this day until your last day on this earth, know that you ARE the very best version of you which means nobody can be a better you than you!

Say 2 Self: Until I know WHO I am and WHOSE I am, I can't possibly know my purpose, my potential or WHAT rightfully belongs to me.

Your Due Inheritance

"But to all who did receive Him, who believed His name, He gave the right to become children of God."
John 1:12 ESV

According to scripture, if you are a born-again believer/child of God, regardless of race or ethnicity, you are joint heirs with Christ and justly 'entitled' to a plethora of amazing benefits from our Father God. I'm extremely glad that He is no respecter of persons, and that He is a whosoever/whatsoever kind of God!

> *"For verily I say unto you, that whosoever shall say unto this mountain, be thou removed, and be thou cast into the sea; and shall not doubt in his heart but shall believe that those things which he saith shall come to pass; he shall have whatsoever he saith."* **Mark 11:23 KJV**

Social Media is just as full of posts about white 'privilege' as it is posts about 'entitlement'. One group uses white 'privilege' as a platform while the other uses 'entitlement' and between the two, the racist saga continues. Even so, you know what they say, "There are three sides to every story: yours, mine and the truth." Well, the truth is that we *all* have an inheritance from God, and we are *all* 'privileged' to be 'entitled' to His promises.

But exactly what does it mean to be an heir? Webster defines an heir as a person legally 'entitled' to the property or rank of another on that person's death.

So, when Jesus died, we became heirs to all that was rightfully his based on him being the Son of God.

As heirs, one of the attributes we have is His glory (inner brightness, brilliance and ability to shine). **Romans 8:17** NIV reads, *"And since we are His children, we are His heirs. In fact, together with Christ we are heirs of God's glory."* We should be lights shining brightly in this dark world. We should be <u>thinking</u>, <u>living</u>, <u>talking</u> and <u>walking</u> like His children: boldly, uprightly and proudly … undoubtedly both privileged and entitled. LOL - Ha, Ha devil.

Here's just a foretaste of your God-given birthright privileges and entitlements …

Communion with God	Boldness & Confidence
Divine Health & Wealth	Access to the Throne
Deliverance from evil	Spiritual Gifts & Talents
Divine Protection	Blessings (multiplied possessions)
Forgiveness of Sin	Grace and Mercy
Divine Purpose	Peace that surpasses all understanding
Kingdom Authority	Unmerited Favor
Divine Revelation	The Gift of Eternal Life
God's Unconditional Love	Wisdom and Knowledge
Divine Provision	Victory over death, hell & the grave

What this means for God's Children is that when life throws us a curve ball, we don't have live in fear, tuck tail and hide or even contemplate giving up. We always win in the end!

Therefore, when we are faced with feelings of defeat and despair, we must remember that our Father God loves us dearly and is in full control which guarantees our triumphant outcome. We must learn to rely on His ability and His promise to make our temporarily devastating blows and disappointments, somehow, workout for our good. And finally, even though it *don't* feel good, we should trust that it will turn out *for* the good. All these mind-full acts help us to not crumble, but to stand strong in the face of adversity.

> *"He will wipe every tear from their eyes. There will be no more death or mourning or crying or pain, for the old order of things has passed away."* **Revelation 21:4**

Consequently, as heirs, we are yet able to anticipate an abundant life even after the death of a loved one, a bitter divorce, a terminal diagnosis, a natural disaster, corporate layoffs, financial setbacks, political unrest, tragic accidents and backstabbing setups.

Yes, in this life you will surely have trouble, but my friend please make a mental note of these two things:

1) Tough times don't last; God's people do.

2) That which you don't allow to break you makes you better, stronger and wiser.

Once you fully understand and embrace the magnitude of God's goodness and glory awaiting you, you are better able to endure whatever comes your way. Likewise, you should always praise God. Ever so powerful is a deliberate decision to praise Him smack dab in the middle of trials and tribulations as a demonstration and proclamation of your faith. When you go through muster up a praise on the inside of you and watch burdens lift and the peace, presence and power of God take over. How about we stop right here – right now - and take us a praise break?! Google Isaac Carree's song **In the Middle** & William Murphy's **It's Working**. ⍰

Nothing pleases God more than knowing that His children trust Him to do what He said He would do. His written word is your insurance and assurance that you will receive all He has promised. Your faith and trust please Him!

> *"God is not a man, so he does not lie. He is not human, so he does not change his mind. Has he ever spoken and failed to act? Has he ever promised and not carried it through?"* **Numbers 23:19**

Several years ago, my dearest childhood friend fell suddenly ill. It took a long drawn out series of doctor visits, hospital stays, inpatient tests, outpatient treatments and prescription drug trials to figure out what was going wrong in her body. At younger than 40 years of age, she was beyond devastated, riddled with pain and physically bedridden when I visited her. This loving mother, devoted wife, anointed prayer warrior and lifelong confidant of mine was waging the battle of a lifetime and God allowed me to show up in the nick of time to help her fight.

When I arrived, her daughters braced me for what I would see … my strong and courageous sister, lying on a malicious bed of affliction, slipping in and out of consciousness at the command of the numerous drugs dominating her weakened body.

Their focus had been slyly shifted from fighting, resisting and using scripture against its brutal ramifications to study every commentary they could find on the two diseases day in and day out. With great remorse they informed me of her 'accepted and anticipated' inevitable disabled state. Filled with despair, they explained what to expect, when to expect it, every possible complication, how long symptoms would last and every known side effect. Impressively, they were talking the clinical talk like professionals. As loving caregivers, they dutifully and lovingly shared brushing her teeth, combing her hair, dressing her and pushing her around in a wheelchair.

My jaws dropped and heart sank from the shocking account of it all. "Why Lord? Why her? Why now, she's not even forty?" I gently opened the bedroom door as she was trying to cheer up and gather up enough strength to greet me with a smile. Her shallow voice uttered, "Hey girl."

Leaning over to embrace her tightly, and from the depths of my heart attempting to transfer some of my vitality into the very core of her being, I fought back my tears enough to mumble "Heeeeeey girl." When we separated, I noticed a large basket of prescription medications in bottles of varied sizes on the nightstand and that her bed was hidden in books … like 15-20 books!!!

We began moving them out of the way to clear a space for me to sit down next to her. "Girl, what are all of these books for?" I asked in concerned amazement. "I'm reading up on what the doctors finally found out I have," she explained as she started to tear up.

Without saying another word, I picked up the first book to see what the diagnosis was: *Lyme Brain: The Impact of Lyme Disease on Your Brain.* How strange it felt to see a non-Christian theme or title on the cover; that's all she ever read other than the Bible itself.

Shaken by her frailty, I curiously reached out for a second book: *The Everything Guide to Lyme Disease.* What?! Another one?! I looked at her in shocking disbelief as she eagerly handed me the next book like a child would his/her favorite toys with a playmate: *Bite Me: How Lyme Disease Stole My Childhood, Made Me Crazy, and Almost Killed Me.*

Somehow the look in her eyes spoke what she wanted me to know … just how bad it was and how overwhelmed by this sickness she'd been.

Having me look at the books which had now become her life's story was her way of including me in the acceptance of her rapidly declining condition. What in the world had happened to my sister-friend?

Looking through the other stack of titles on fibromyalgia was more than my spirit could tolerate. It all seemed so surreal. My breaths shortened. The room felt hot; it started closing in on me. I felt faint. I needed air.

"God what is going on here? Talk to me, please," I silently pleaded. "Go to the restroom, and I will give you instructions," He calmly replied.

I excused myself and couldn't wait to shut the bathroom door. Whew! I could breathe again. "Lord, what is this?" I asked in desperation. "Oppression, depression, deception and a strong spirit of infirmity which has been accepted and permitted to dominate - run rampant." He explained. "But how?

I know for a fact that everyone in this household is anointed, they are mighty in you, covered by the Blood and chosen by you. They unashamedly and faithfully live for you Lord. They are yours! I've seen you do so many miraculous wonders for them and through them; why are you allowing this debilitating attack?" I rambled and tried to reason with Him. His response was priceless. "I allowed it to show up, but she has given it permission to continue," He calmly declared.

Dumbfounded by the revelation, I had no more words. Silence prevailed. Then the reality hit me ... "Wow! She's accepted it as permanent ... OMG!! She has a say so in this!

She has dominion to overcome this *thang*!!"

God's message was short but ever so clear. He basically told me that the attack came upon her as a test of faith; at some point, she accepted it and continued to grant it access by surrendering her power. At any moment she simply could choose to exercise her authority in faith to receive healing.

The truth was that she had power over her situation all along although her body, the books and doctor's reports all presented facts dictating otherwise. The enemy had unknowingly been granted free access ... he was in like Flynn; freely destroying the entire family's quality of life while deceptively destroying any hopes of a testimony about the healing power they all possessed.

Like a wilted plant freshly watered and placed in the sunlight to bask, I perked up, washed my hands and prepared for war. Super charged to share the good news, I knew it was time to go to battle in the Spirit and stand in the gap with her to fight off this evil, unclean and tormenting spirit of infirmity using God's word and the Blood of Jesus.

Instead of just walking back into her bedroom, I closed shut her opened door and then knocked on it. Not knowing what I was up to, she asked, "Girl why did you close my door, and why are you out there knocking? Come on in." I told her I wanted to play a game we played when we were in elementary school called "Knock, Knock. Who's There?"

She gently smiled saying, "Girl, you're so crazy! Come on in here, I don't feel like playing." I chuckled and told her that she had to play it with me. "After all, the Bible says laughter is medicine for your soul." She shook her head and lightly laughed before telling me, "Ok, I'll try."

"Great, so girl when I knock you say who's there, and then tell me to come in." I instructed. "Ready? Here goes." I knocked on the door. She asked, "Who's there?" I said, "Lyme disease. Now tell me to come in." She did.

I opened the door, came in and saw a half grin with scrunched brows on her face. I walked out and shut the door back quickly only to start knocking again.

"Who's there?" she asked. "Fibromyalgia. Now tell me to come in." She did. Once more I opened the door and came in. By now she was trying to hold back her laughter. Walking right back out and back in again, we repeated this until she had let Lyme disease, fibromyalgia, and every associated miserable symptom I could think of come into her room.

After about 15 minutes of this Divine craze, a hysterical healing laughter filled the house. In fact, the merriment from this revelation rang so loud, her daughters ran upstairs to see witness the delirium. I explained what God had revealed to me, and they were all as astonished as I'd been.

He was right! Admittedly, every one of them had totally accepted the diagnosis and by believing the facts staring them in the face had given it carte blanche accepting it as her new normal. **But God!** Determined not to see my best friend suffer in this condition **NOT 1 MORE DAY** – I told the enemy, "Game over!"

Boldly, I instructed the girls to pack up all the books and return them to the library from whence they'd come. My friend sat and watched in amazement trying to justify keeping a few at hand for reference. "Absolutely not! The devil is a liar. Girl, all that you don't know by now, you don't need to know.

The only thing you will be reading from this day forth is the Word of God. You must meditate and marinate on healing scriptures day and night. No more of this madness," I confidently advised. She agreed, and we laughed once more at the simplicity of it all. "Really God … Knock, Knock?!" LOL

Thumbing through her basket of over the counter and prescription drugs, the 12 bottles of pills looked like the perfect recipe for an early death to me. Diligently and deliberately, I read each label, and considered each ingredient.

Among the parade of pharmaceutical concoctions were Ambien, Flexeril, Soma, Naproxen, Hydrocodone, and a host of interesting others. What gave tremendous validity to this part of my divinely timed visit was the fact that despite the plethora of sleep aids, pain relievers, energy/mood boosters, muscle relaxers and elixirs, pain persisted, and sleep evaded her.

What?! Go figure.

At the prompting and leading of the Holy Spirit, I was able to discern meds with overlapping functions, contraindications and combinations which were extremely toxic to her system. Stepping out in faith, she trusted the newly exposed truths and eliminated all but three … discontinuing nine of them completely until her next doctor's visit. **(PLEASE DO NOT ATTEMPT THIS ON YOUR OWN)**

We thanked God profusely for granting us wisdom and knowledge in a family group prayer following the removal of the books and excess meds. We reminded Him of who she was, whose she was and her right to a healthy, disease-free life as we touched and agreed with His promise/ability to heal, set free and deliver. We boldly declared that by Jesus' stripes she was already healed, that no weapon formed against her would prosper and commanded Satan to take his hands off. God gave us a list of foods for her to add daily to her diet and others to eliminate. In tears of joy and thanksgiving we ended our visit.

It was on and poppin' once the power of God had been released. **NOT 1 MORE DAY** did she dwell on her sickness or succumb to the symptoms of disease in her body. **NOT 1 MORE DAY** was she bound and rendered helpless by the spirit of infirmity. The weeks and months to come would prove God faithful.

As always, He answered our prayers and turned her pain, suffering and infirmity into a testimony for others. In fact, the team of baffled doctors asked her what she was doing differently when she returned for visits because her prognosis kept changing for the better with each appointment. All glory and praises be to God!

A refocused mindset on healing rather than sickness, spiritual realignment with the Word of God, child-like obedience and trust in her Creator is all it took to unlock the door to her physical breakthrough. Peace of mind, sweet rest, self-reliance, full mobility and complete restoration were her inheritance. You too are entitled and privileged to receive supernatural healing and deliverance.

> **Say 2 Self:** When I know what belongs to me, I can readily and boldly reject and denounce that which does not.

Your True Importance

I love music … many kinds of music, and when I think about our importance to God, Patti LaBelle's - *If Only You Knew* song lyrics come to mind. Yes, He loves you! Almighty God, The Great I AM, The Creator of the Universe, The Beginning and The End, and the sovereign, omnipresent, omnipotent Good Shepherd loves Y-O-U. Take a minute to absorb that … The One with all power in His hands, loves you, and He wants you to know it today.

Most importantly, the fact that He loves you guarantees that you gotta be somebody special! You are important.

Now, I realize firsthand that life can put you in some dark lonely situations where you feel like no one loves you or even cares about you, but GOD. Please pause and go to this link: https://www.youtube.com/watch?v=qpSE3eZTCNo

"For I know the plans I have for you," says the LORD. "They are plans for good and not for disaster, to give you a future and a hope." **Jerimiah 29:11 NLT**

He has a plan for your life. His plan for you is not just any plan … not a one size fits all kind of deal, but a perfect plan and purpose designed with your unique **TAGs** and desires in mind. A plan to give you His best and to use you for His glory. He wants to show you off to the rest of the world as His Beloved in whom He is well pleased.

He's not asking for your perfection; He loves you as you are. He's asking for you to allow Him to walk and talk with you, to be your Lord and Savior and invite Him into your circumstances. Learn to trust Him in all things …

always.

Truthfully, the more complicated, embarrassing and jacked up you think things are, the more glory He will get when He makes the crooked places straight for you. Everyone will see and know that God is at work on your behalf.

It is His greatest desire to bless you abundantly, give you His Kingdom here on earth, satisfy your mouth with good things and communicate with you daily. Seek Him while He may be found …

He is patiently waiting for you to call Him Abba Father.

He wants a personal relationship with you!

What are you waiting for?

Don't let **NOT 1 MORE DAY** go by without making a decision to know your Father, trust Him and learn to hear His voice. Today is the day, if you have not done so already, to accept His Son Jesus into your heart.

(SSI) Soul Self Inventory:

1. Are my beliefs/values mine or someone else's?

2. Who's report or words have I believed until today?

3. Where did my self-esteem (or lack of it) come from?

4. What/who have I accepted and allowed into my life as a result of not understanding who and whose I am?

5. Now that I know my identity, my inheritance and my importance to God's purpose and plan, what will I do differently?

<u>Prayer 2 Pray Today</u>:

Heavenly Father,

I believe in you and your Son Jesus Christ. I believe that you raised Him from the dead and that He is seated at your right hand. I ask Him now to come into my heart and be my personal savior, to free me from my sins and cleanse me from all unrighteousness. Now Lord, I realize that I've been lost without you in my life and unsure of who I was to you until now. I had no idea how much you love me, and I am in awe of the wonderful things you must have planned for my life.

Thank you for loving me. Thank you for the thoughts that you have towards me to give me an expected end. Thank you for being my Father, my Lord, my God, my strength when I was weak and my comforter in times of pain. Thank you for opening my eyes of understanding and for letting me know that I don't have to settle for less than I deserve **NOT 1 MORE DAY**, *and that I am entitled to the best because I belong to You.*

Thank you for leading me into the truth of who I am and whose I am, so that I can begin to receive all that You have prepared for me. Thank you for your healing power, your living word and your provision. Thank you for choosing me to let my light shine before others and glorify you. Thank you for not letting my enemies triumph over me and for granting me the gift of eternal life through your Son Jesus Christ.

Amen.

CHAPTER 3

Blessed Assurance & Assistance

"Seek ye first the Kingdom of God and all His righteousness and all these things will be added unto you." **Matthew 6:33**

Poverty, sickness, suffering and disease do NOT belong to us as believers. Do these intruders exist? Do they show up in our lives? You bet they do, but there is a method to the madness and an explanation for their continuation.

John 10:10, Jesus warns about the thief who comes only to steal, kill and destroy, but He also informs that He has come so we can have life and have it more abundantly. Exactly what does an abundant life look like? Does it mean that there will be no problems, no sickness, no hardships, no disappointments, no setbacks or set ups?

Nope, not at all.

The word 'abundant' in the Greek language is 'perisson' which means – exceedingly, beyond measure, far more than expected or anticipated, very superfluous.

An abundant life is one of indescribable peace, joy, mercy, wisdom, grace, favor and unconditional love from our Heavenly Father despite whatever else may be going on. Money cannot buy any of those blessed assurances; they are gifts.

When the Bible speaks of an abundant life it is referring to the blessed assurance that is ours when we focus our energies and efforts on kingdom building: loving God, edifying one another, setting a Godlike example via our thoughts-words-deeds, and serving in some capacity as a blessing to others. Choosing to believe (even in the face of adversity) that the Greater One lives inside of us and will equip us with what we need to overcome.

If you're like me, you want to live a life that overflows with God's goodness, mercy, love, favor, peace and joy … an abundant life. Unfortunately, there are days that we find ourselves amid life's chaos and confusion which, if we allow it to, can cause us to feel less than blessed.

There will be times of financial hardship - times of lack and uncertainty – times of spiritual drought where it seems like God has forgotten about our labors of love and sacrifices of praise. Even worse, there will be moments of deep emotional despair, and seemingly unbearable loneliness.

It is in these uncomfortable and unfortunate times that God wants us (His children) to call, to cry out and lean on Him … to seek His face, His will and His way. Take a look at this prescription for receiving total healing from God:

> *"If my people, who are called by my name, will humble themselves and pray and seek my face and turn from their wicked ways, then I will hear from heaven, and I will forgive their sin and will heal their <u>land</u>."* **2 Chronicles 7:14**

In this passage, when it refers to <u>land</u>, it's talking about whatever belongs to you that needs to be made whole, restored or set aright: your children, personal/professional relationships, finances, self-image, marriage, health, your mind and the list goes on and on. He is patiently waiting for you to invite Him into your situation and circumstances.

Unfortunately, in times of disappointment, we don't call His name – we don't call on Him – we call on other people … people with limited thinking and resources who can't even help or salvage themselves because of internal struggles with their own issues. Don't get me wrong here, I value friendship and have several dear friends whom I believe are loyal to me and vice versa. I also thank God for my family and love them deeply.

However, I've learned to respect the frailty of humanity, and so should you. Everyone has their own limitations, problems, issues and means of treading through the troubled waters of life. Oft times it's nothing personal, and as well intended as some may be when you reach out to them, please understand that: your secrets may not be safe, your pain may bring them a sick sense of pleasure and your temporary trial may be permanently held over your head long after the storm is over.

I don't want you to be disillusioned **NOT 1 MORE DAY.**

Embrace this truth. Get set free from depending on the undependable; become intentional and call upon The One.

The One who created you,

The One who thought you were worth dying for,

The One who will never leave you nor forsake you,

The One who will build you up and strengthen you,

The One who protects you from dangers seen/unseen,

The One who can make a way out of no way,

The One who knows you better than you know yourself,

The _only_ One who CANNOT lie/will NOT fail and -

Say 2 Self: My God favors me. He knows my name!

Let's study this powerful example from ***Psalm18:6-20:***

6 In my distress I called upon the LORD, and cried unto my God:

he heard my voice out of his temple, and my cry came before him,

even into his ears.

7 Then the earth shook and trembled; the foundations also of the

hills moved and were shaken, because he was wroth.

8 There went up a smoke out of his nostrils,

and fire out of his mouth devoured: coals were kindled by it.

9 He bowed the heavens also and came down:

and darkness was under his feet.

10 And he rode upon a cherub, and did fly: yea,

he did fly upon the wings of the wind.

11 He made darkness his secret place; his pavilion round

about him were dark waters and thick clouds of the skies.

12 At the brightness that was before him his thick clouds passed,

hail stones and coals of fire.

13 The LORD also thundered in the heavens, and the

Highest gave his voice; hail stones and coals of fire.

14 Yea, he sent out his arrows, and scattered them;

and he shot out lightnings and discomfited them.

15 Then the channels of waters were seen, and the foundations

of the world were discovered at thy rebuke, O LORD,

at the blast of the breath of thy nostrils.

16 He sent from above, he took me, he drew me out of many waters.

17 He delivered me from my strong enemy,

and from them which hated me: for they were too strong for me.

18 They prevented me in the day of my calamity: but the LORD was my stay.

19 He brought me forth also into a large place;
he delivered me, because he delighted in me.

20 The LORD rewarded me according to my righteousness;
according to the cleanness of my hands hath he recompensed me.

In this passage, David called upon the Lord and cried unto his God. Did you see how God showed up and showed out for His child? God was visibly upset by the plight of David (His Child) and boy did He hastily come to the rescue. Isn't that the same love, fierceness and fury that most parents have for their children when in distress? What an incredible witness of God's promise to protect/deliver when you call.

Additionally, Jesus provides us with words of comfort to prepare us and steady us before trouble comes …

"I have told you all this so that in Me you may have peace. Here on earth you will have many trials and sorrows. But take courage, I have overcome the world." **John 16:33**

He further assures in **John 14: 12-14:**

Say 2 Self:
When I'm under attack, I know God has my back; I will NOT be defeated!

Flashback One:

2006 started off quite well. Early January, I was blessed with the home of my dreams. Mid-February, I purchased my first Mercedes Benz (dream vehicle) ... a shiny and sporty silver ML320. Blessings were abounding and I couldn't have been happier, more inspired or motivated to continue dreaming new dreams, setting bigger goals and aiming higher to reach them. Yes, life was good! My progress, prosperity and professional status looked promising Alas, everything appeared to work in my favor.

However, one weekend in March, God forewarned me of an upcoming change in my career. My little brother,

John, who had spent the weekend with me, was awakened by the smell of oven-crisped bacon, fresh hot buttermilk biscuits, and possibly a whiff of buttery garlic-cheese grits. The sound of his footsteps let me know it wouldn't be long before he joined me downstairs.

Leisurely descending one step at a time, rubbing his eyes and shaking his head, from under the hairdryer beaming blasts of fire on my forehead and neck, I looked up. He said, "Good morning Jacq, OMG, I can't. I'm going back upstairs!"

Beyond puzzled by his comment and knowing how he looked forward to my home cooking, I said "Huh? That doesn't make sense. You get up, start down the stairs and then say you're going back up? John please … I knooowww you are ready to eat!" I tooted. He was my biggest culinary fan, someone who seriously loved my cooking and always had an alarmingly robust appetite.

Still looking wide-eyed and forlorn, he said, "I have to go back upstairs Jacq because I don't like what I see." Utterly frustrated at this point I asked, "What are you talking about?" He gave me that pitiful look I'd get whenever embarrassment overshadowed his desire to tell me something. He attempted to speak then paused.

"What is it?" I insisted. "Jacq, I've seen you sitting in that very spot, under the hairdryer in a vision, but the table was full of sheets of paper just like it is now. "Okay and…," I impatiently blurted out. "What's the big deal about that?" He paused again. Becoming extremely irritated, I huffed, "John, are you going to tell me or not?" I hated when he would drag his thoughts and words out like this … Ugh. He gingerly walked down a few steps then stopped, leaned over the rail and with tears in his eyes he said, "Jacq, I saw you losing your job, and you working from home."

I immediately retorted, "Well, I don't receive that at all. The devil is a liar! Plus, even if it did happen, I know I'd still be ok … God's got my back!" He looked relieved, proceeded down the few remaining stairs, entered the kitchen and piled his plate up with so much food it looked like he would never finish eating.

Intentionally ignoring the fact, at that moment, that John was a visionary whom God had shown numerous prophetic visions, I snickered to myself and continued filling out the pile of product order forms in front of me.

Flashback Two: Now what had happened was (lol) - by early 2006, the "dot.com" industry had taken quite a hit in the stock market, and economically the future wasn't looking too bright. In fact, the successful and renowned computer software company, which had been my employer since 1997 (just two months short of ten years) was now in its second fiscal year of exercising their 'at will' right to lay off employees throughout our global organization.

Quarter after stressful quarter, desks would suddenly appear empty, phone extensions rang to no avail, email addresses mysteriously got deleted from the database, and the fear of pink slips ran rampant. Sure enough, God had indeed given my little brother an in-time word for me.

That advanced notice of what was about to happen just two months later, cushioned what would have otherwise felt like a cruel wrecking ball drop. Well, unfortunately, May was my month.

On May 8th of 2006, the morning of my last day in corporate America, Yolanda Adams' song, *"It's Gon' Be Nice"* was blasting from my CD player as I pulled into the six-story parking garage of the prestigious Fortune 500 company I had been working at for nearly a decade. After parking on the 4th floor in my usual corner spot, I rode the elevator down the lobby level, walked into the incredible main lobby where a black baby grand piano played as employees rushed in and out of the Starbucks perfectly positioned inside of the onsite restaurant just to the right of the company elevators. Foregoing a tempting aromatic cup of Java, I headed towards them, pressed the up button and awaited the opening of doors.

Stepping inside, I was greeted by decorative floor to ceiling, brown, black and white spotted genuine cowhide walls. I pressed the button for the twentieth level and rode smoothly up to the top of my, Proud to Be a Texan, corporate headquarter building just as I'd done for many years prior.

Passing the call center team, speaking to those who weren't on a call and nodding with a smile to others who were, I reached my cozy cubicle. When I attempted to log into my phone (which also served as our electronic timekeeper) I heard a series of flat fast-busy signals. That's weird I recall thinking to myself. I tried again … still flat fast-busy beeps. No sooner than I dialed the four-digit login code for the third time, I noticed someone approaching me; it was a senior manager from another location on the east coast. She and I established a hugging rapport over the years, so I quickly jumped to greet her in our usual manner – with a hug. Unexpectedly, with a weird, rigid and very reserved stance, I felt her walls go up.

Taking a deep breath as my body temperature chilled in response to the coldness radiating from the pupils of her eyes, my spirit somersaulted deep within the pit of my stomach. I knew without a doubt … it was my turn.

Laid off.

There I was less than two hours after pulling into the parking garage, cranking up my 'dream vehicle', leaving my 'incredible' corporate job, and heading back to my 'dream' home. The end of *"It's Gon' Be Nice"* was still playing when I started up the engine to drive out for the last time. Basking in the infinite wisdom and forewarning of the Holy Spirit via John, I opened the sunroof, hit rewind, turned up the volume even louder, and sang at the top of my lungs. Crying and thanking God profusely, I jammed all the way back home.

My God softened what could have been sheer devastation when He showed my little brother, months prior, the first and only time I'd ever been laid off.

When I arrived home, I collapsed on my couch and attempted to wrap my mind around the facts: I was single, unemployed with no savings and no backup plan. Desperately needing to share this unwelcomed moment, I did what most grown people do when faced with a crisis … I called my mother.

As I gave her a minute by minute rundown of my morning, on the other end of the phone I heard sorrowful sighs and expression after expression of utter disbelief which eventually resulted in her maternal attempt to comfort me. In a disappointed, yet somewhat reassuring, voice she said, "Well I guess you just have to put your things in storage, come live with me and start over from there." Sadly, those weren't the words I wanted or needed to hear. As kind and as heartfelt as her offer sounded, a dose of hope in my ability to survive and thrive on my own was what the doctor ordered. I thanked her, and when we got off the phone, I cried out to God just like David did.

I turned my face upwards with tears streaming down my cheeks and snot running from my nostrils into my plea-filled mouth. Looking at the lovely high vaulted ceilings in the home He'd blessed me with just four months prior, and lifted my hands to God:

"Father, I stretch my hands unto Thee, no other help do I know. In Jesus' name Lord God have mercy on me and forgive me for my sins and whatever I may have done displeasing in your sight. Lord God, I know you knew this day was coming long before I did. You knew it when you formed me in my mother's womb. You knew it when you blessed me with this house. You knew it when you allowed me to get the vehicle of my dreams and your word promises me that the blessings that come from you maketh rich and added no sorrow.

I don't believe you brought me this far to have me lose it all. I know you didn't bring me this far to leave me. So, Lord I trust you. And Lord, I know you can do exceedingly abundantly above and beyond anything I

It felt strange waking up the next morning without someplace to go, a title to uphold or a reason to get out of bed, so I didn't. After a few dazed days, I began to ask myself what I really wanted to do next with my life and my career. Entrepreneurship was once again on the horizon, but what kind of business would it be? So many choices.

Too many options. Decisions, decisions and more decisions.   I took my time deliberating and explored several MLM opportunities that held the promise of time and financial freedom. I was especially drawn in by the dynamic motivational talks, diverse team demographics, lucrative compensation plans and the ability to make my own schedule. Let freedom ring … let freedom ring, my soul was ignited, and I was excited!

Not too long into my professionally dormant state, the effects of being on my own started to sink in. After a night of feeling terribly alone and having fallen asleep by flooding my pillow with tears as I sought God for love and companionship, I felt hungover. Somehow, the thought of having someone in my life to talk to and share in this unprecedented season loomed heavily in my heart. I longed for someone to love who loved me back.

While driving down Hwy 6 with my sunroof open the following morning, cruising, swaying and listening to Yolanda Adams' 'Be Blessed', I basked in the bright sunshine. Loving the warm yet breezy fresh June air, worshipping God, crying like a baby and singing to the top of my lungs I rode on.

Then suddenly, out of the corner of my tear laden eyes, I saw a lady selling puppies on the side of the busy roadway. "How cute," I thought as I kept driving past, but felt the Holy Spirit say, *"Turn around Jacq."*

Smiling now through my tears, I retorted, "Really God?! A dog?! You've got jokes!" Gently, He repeated … *"Turn around."* Trying to clarify my intention I replied, "A man Lord, not a dog. A man is what I was crying about. I want a man. I don't want no dog." *"Turn around."* He said firmly for the third time. "Lord you can't be serious … are you?" I asked continuing to drive ahead in disbelief. "OMG, you really want me to get a dog huh Lord?!" I reaffirmed from deep within my failing resistance.

Obediently, I made a quick U-turn and headed back towards the roadside puppy sale. I slowly rolled up, got out and walked up to the cage of the most adorable baby pugs I'd ever seen. There he was - beige with a little black trimmed mouth, staring at me with the biggest, cutest black eyes - flooding my lonely heart with warm fuzzies.

Talk about unexpectedly mesmerizing, like that insanely infatuated high you get with love at first sight! "But wait, how much was he?" I wondered, then dared to ask.

"Five-hundred dollars," the lady proudly replied. "Ok, this is ridiculous. I don't have a job, a kennel, a doggie bed, puppy food or anything remotely canine related, and I'm standing here about to throw five bills away on a dog? No way! The devil is a liar; this ain't You God. I'm tripping."

"Well, thanks but no thanks ma'am," I said emphatically as I began to walk off even more discouraged for having wasted my time. Mumbling, "Lord, talk about crazy. Now that was crazy, but I know that wasn't You, I'm not crazy. The devil is trying to confuse me. The puppy was cute, and that pit stop You had me make to look at him broke up the pity party I was having, but nah. The last thing I need is a messy dog to feed, clean up after and cost me more money each month. Plus, Lord I don't have a job or a man to help me with any of it remember?"

At the end of my ranting and rationalizing, a still small voice reminded me of words He'd spoken to me many years prior,

"Don't let what you don't have, keep you from getting what I have for you. You said you wanted love and companionship, so there he is Jacq." "Ugggh! Lord, come on now. You knew what kind of companionship I was talking about! I meant a man, a husband, a person to love … not a dog. This ain't funny!" Just then, with my left foot inside of the car, right before I shut the door, the lady yelled, "Wait Miss, I will let you have that one you seem to really like for four-hundred." I knew I'd lost the battle.

Looking back at those big black puppy-dog eyes and his innocent little smashed face, I realized that an awe-struck mushiness had completely distorted my thinking, penetrated my heart and destroyed my resolve. Not to mention the insistence coming from the leading of the Holy Spirit and that still small voice.

Shaking my head in defeat, I headed to the nearest ATM, withdrew the money and rushed back to get him. I handed her the equivalent of my next month's light bill, and she gave me a snack-sized Ziploc bag of puppy food, kennel papers and my new little canine companion. That's all I had. Apparently, I didn't need anything else but Bentley.

As I looked down at him, sniffing and exploring the floor of my Benz, I chuckled. "You're a cutie, but you better not even think about peeing in here!" I warned. He didn't.

He was simply adorable with the most friendly, loving and joyful personality. Not surprisingly, God was spot on with His prompting. Being Bentley's mommy was the perfect loneliness cure, and he was indeed the perfect companion. In fact, Bentley and I fared well together until his untimely passing years later one sorrowfully scorching, 105 degrees, summer's day when my father who suffered from dementia, let him out to play in the backyard.

NOT 1 MORE DAY did I have a need to pray to God for companionship!

However, by September, four months post-layoff, an entirely new emotion barged in to interrupt my bliss – the fear of poverty. I found myself obsessively checking my bank account, terrified from watching my eleven-thousand net dollars of severance pay I'd been given back in May disappear. Daily, like a bite of sweet cotton candy, it rapidly dissolved. Relentless monthly expenses demanded mad respect even though I'd drastically cut out a significant amount of my pre-layoff non-essential expenditures.

My then youngest Godchild was fourteen-months old; whenever she stayed with me during the week, and I had to work my $15 per hr/15 hours-a-week job, I would take her to an at-home provider near me. Ms. Nora took incredible care of my precious NaeNae for only one hundred dollars per week which would have been a steal of a deal under different circumstances.

Truth is, when I dropped my baby-girl off on this Monday morning, I would only have a few coins in my ashtray and several crisp two-dollar bills tucked away to last me until Friday's payday.

Backing out of Ms. Nora's driveway one morning after dropping of my baby girl and placing five-twenty dollar bills her in hand, the enemy of faith (**RAL**) *reason and logic*, whispered in my ear ... "You are the biggest fool, you know you can't afford to be keeping this baby, you have full-time bills and a part-time job. Look at you, you really don't have any money left to take care of yourself."

It was a semi-factual taunting. I couldn't afford it, but I knew she was better off with me than not, and regardless the cost I loved her dearly. Mine was a sacrifice of love which I insisted on making, yet for all practical purposes, (**RAL**) sounded right.

Before I could turn the corner, I heard the voice of God softly instruct me. ***"Jacq, I want you to think about money like you think about air."*** Just as though a buzzing bee was zooming around my head, I shook it quickly from left to right in downright confusion before our dialogue began. "Huh, Lord? What do you mean like I think about air?" Chuckling at the thought, I continued, "I don't think about air." ***"Exactly, you don't think about air,"*** He calmly replied. ***"Yet, without it you wouldn't be alive,"*** He continued.

I still didn't get it. "Lord, it's too early in the morning for this deep talk. I don't know what you are saying to me and I'm getting frustrated." It felt like I was in some weird drunken stupor because His words were usually not this difficult to comprehend.

"I'm trying, but I don't get it Lord?! I have never thought about air." I slurred deliriously. "Money like air?! Help me understand what you're saying to me?" I fumbled.

Honestly, it was so off-putting that I chalked it up to a spirit of confusion scrambling up the message and causing me to miss the whatever point the Holy Spirit attempted to make. "Lord, I can't make sense of what you are saying. This can't be you. Satan, I rebuke you in the name of Jesus!"

Once again, very patiently … God spoke, ***"You don't think about air, yet you must have it to live. Without it you will die. You don't think about it, you just breathe, and it's there."*** Suddenly, His message became crystal clear to me. His words and analogy, so profoundly assuring and liberating made me weep. Tears like raindrops on a windowsill rolled down my face in sheer gratitude of what He was saying. I released the stress and pressure of financial limitations with each tear I shed.

God knew I'd been frantically (at times obsessively) looking at my bank account balance 5-10 times a day to see what posted, what was pending and how much money remained. Watching it dwindle had become nerve wrecking. The fear of poverty and lack ruled my every waking hour and had me living in financial bondage. My God spoke life into the driest season of my life and gave me permission to just live and trust Him fully to provide what I needed without anxiously fretting over every dollar spent. With great enthusiasm, I began rehearsing the revelation He'd given: *"Just live. As I breathe in the air He so faithfully and freely supplies, trust Him to provide the finances I need to keep living. Think about money like I think about air ... don't! Just live and breathe (inhale/exhale) knowing He – Jehovah Jireh - will provide."*

Yes! At that moment, I received true financial freedom. **NOT 1 MORE DAY** was I tormented by doubt, fear or anxiety regarding His ability to fill/overflow my cup (bank account). Even though I continued to be responsible with my money, I did not compulsively check the balance, I just breathed and exhaled trusting Him to do just as He promised.

Noticeably, the anxious thoughts of poverty, lack, running out money or not having enough vanished. All residue of the heavy disquieting burden of my pending insufficient self-sufficiency lifted the moment I accepted

His powerful word into my spirit. Instantly delivering me from a suffocating fear of poverty, God gave me blessed assurance.

Despite the little pay I earned from week to week, I had a peace that surpassed my understanding because I was living by faith and choosing to rely on His word and His ability instead of my own. Not surprisingly, God held true true to His word. He kept me afloat financially, and I kept keeping NaeNae. Sure enough, the money I had was blessed, and I've not experienced lack or want from that day to this one.

Trust and believe He's able!

> **Say 2 Self:** God, Jehovah Jireh, is my provider; He will show up on time _every time_ for me!

Now watch this … It wasn't until January of the following year (about 8 months after my initial 'laid-off' prayer) that I was sitting upstairs in my home office watching the infamous television evangelist, Rod Parsley, preach. He kept going on and on about vowing a vow to God and describing his burning desire to sow a $10,000 seed offering some day. Rod said when he shared his vision with his wife, she thought of it as a ridiculously generous $10,000 idea.

Nonetheless, his desire wouldn't let him rest, so he decided to anchor his faith on **2 Corinthians 9:10 *"For God is the one who provides seed for the farmer and then bread to eat. In the same way, he will provide and increase your resources and then produce a great harvest of generosity in you." (NIV)*** God put Rod in remembrance of His word and determined in his heart to expect the seed for sowing to manifest. He gives seed to the sower!

Rod's phone began ringing off the hook with one obedient caller after another saying that God told them to plant a seed of faith into His ministry. Within days, the full ten-thousand dollars he vowed miraculously manifested – God provided him with the seed! I listened as he encouraged anyone with a need bigger than they were able to meet, to make a vow unto the Lord and fulfill it by faith.

Down to the last dwindling remains of my severance pay, surviving only on $15 hours a week at $15/hour, I decided I had nothing to lose, literally. Surprisingly, it wasn't until typing this right now that I realized it had been eight months after my layoff. Biblically, the number 8 represents a new beginning. A fresh new start … most definitely!

He called out for Believers to make one thousand-dollar vows. Rod kept inviting us to prove God this day and trust Him to provide the seed to sow, then turn around and bless us for our obedience. It sounded like a solid plan to me.

Knowing God is no respecter of persons, and if He did it for Rod, He'd do it for me, I picked up the phone. Obediently, I made my largest vow ever, a one thousand-dollar faith pledge. My hands were sweating, my heart was beating a million beats per second, and my insides were trembling. This was serious! This was huge! "Okay girl," I thought, "You're wading in some profound spiritual waters, and you know you don't have any money to give. Clearly, you're in way over your head." My entire body felt weak … limp; my flesh was tempted to back out, but I knew I'd done right in God's eyes. I wanted to please Him.

While waiting with great anticipation for God to supply the seed for me to make good on my vow, I kept reminding Him of His word. After about a week or two passed, sheer boredom had set in at home, so I decided to rummage through the medium sized box of my personal belongings that I left with on my last day of Corporate America (8 months prior) back in May 2006.

Reminiscing as I sorted through the pictures, awards, certificates and logo items, I'd either won or been given over the years, I stumbled upon an old letter from Fidelity Investments. We had a matching 401k benefit from the company that I'd taken advantage of over the years, but various unforeseen life and family circumstances forced me to make several loans and hardship withdrawals.

In fact, in October 2005, our company stock dropped big time, and to prevent further losses many of us pulled the bulk of our monies down. Therefore, when I ran across this letter my excitement was not too grand. At best, I anticipated a balance of between five to seven hundred dollars in the portfolio, and I needed it like yesterday. Especially since I'd made an unprecedented vow to God, I wanted whatever remained.

Boldly, I picked up the phone and called Fidelity to make a final withdrawal. After a series of worrisome prompts, a super friendly male representative finally beeped in asking me to verify what seemed like a million security questions. He finally got around to asking what he could do for me. "I'd like to close my account and withdraw all of my current funds please," I stated emphatically.

A long pause ensued before his voice on the other end sounded frantically concerned, "Ma'am, are you sure you don't want to speak to one of our plan advisors first?" Here we go, I thought to myself…it never fails. Drum roll please as they present all this red tape to get my own money. "No, I don't need to speak to anyone other than you. All I want to do is close out this account and get <u>my</u> money that <u>I</u> put into it," I barked. He cleared his throat sensing my irritation. "Ok, well … uh, ma'am, do you want to withdraw the full balance today?" he asked attempting to clarify my intent.

"Sir listen, yes I want all of it! I would like whatever is in there right now sent to me as soon as possible. I don't want to speak to anyone else. I don't feel like I should have to jump through hoops to get my own money. I don't work for the company anymore, and I just want to close this account out please!" I impatiently ranted. After an even longer pause this time, he said, "Miss Jacq, I do understand. Please bear with me just a few more minutes while I place you on hold.

I sighed and rolled my eyes up to the ceiling. "Why does it always take so long to make a withdrawal, if he was setting up my account we'd be done already. How ridiculous … utterly ridiculous." I kept thinking as the hold music played.

After an eternity, he returned to the call. "Miss Jacq, I'm back thanks for your patience. At the close of business yesterday, the market value of your portfolio was $36,760.35 – I'll just need to verify your current banking information to have the funds electronically sent out today."

I held the phone, took it away from my ear, looked at it, put it back, sat up straight and inhaled deeply. "I'm sorry sir, can you please repeat that balance for me?" I asked in a much nicer and far more proper tone. "Sure, it's $36,760.35," he cheerfully advised, and I'll be happy to get that on the way to you with just a few more questions.

OMG!!! Wait. This was crazy! I felt a shout, a scream, a run and a leap coming on. "My God, what have you done? Oh Lord, it's really happening to me just like it did for Rob. You have supplied the seed for my vow and extra for my everyday needs. Ok, whew Lord. Help me Jesus! Breathe Jacq, breathe!" I reminded myself.

"Hello, hello … hello Miss Jacq? Are you there?" he frantically asked. "Uh, yes sir I'm here," I replied from my startled state trying to stay conscious in between the rapid heartbeats pounding profusely within my chest. "Miss Jacq, can you verify your current banking information including the account and routing numbers please?" he kindly asked.   The realization hit me that … I had money, big money which meant I had tons of fresh air to freely breathe! "Hold up, I don't want to close the account after all. I just need the $1,760.35 right now," I calmly retreated. "No problem Ms. Jacq, we will have those funds direct deposited into your account within the next three business days leaving you with a portfolio balance of $35,000. Is there anything else I can help you with today?" Quickly, I assured him, "Uh, no sir. You have been great, thank you!"

Hanging up the phone, I almost passed out frm total astonishment … thank you Jesus! Won't He do it?!

I shared all of that to say this, we serve a mighty God! His word is true, and He NEVER fails to deliver on His promises. He is worthy of your complete trust. Hold on to this truth during the most uncomfortable, unpredictable and undesirable hardships you may have to face. God wants you to know that He will NEVER leave you nor forsake you.

He knows what you have need of before you even ask, and when you do ask, it pleases Him to show up and show out on your behalf. There is nothing too hard for Him, and with Him ALL things are possible! As His biggest fan, advocate and mouthpiece, my sole purpose in writing this book is to encourage you to trust Him.

If you have a financial need, physical ailment, relationship problem or trouble in the workplace, He is waiting. He is willing and He's able to step in - turn things around – make the crooked places straight and right the wrongs in your life. BUT … you must call upon Him.

> *"You want something but don't get it. You kill and covet, but you cannot have what you want. You quarrel and fight. You do not have, because you do not ask God." **James 4:2 (NIV)***

Invite Him into your finances and adverse circumstances.

He's no respecter of persons.

What He's done for me, He will do for you.

He loves you …

you don't have to suffer in silence **NOT 1 MORE DAY**!

(SSI) Soul Self Inventory:

1) In times of financial difficulties do you turn to God?
2) If not, who or what do you turn to and why?
3) Do you trust God to take care of you/your family?
4) Do you *really* believe He can, and He will?
5) Have you mistakenly made your job your God?
6) Do you think it guarantees you financial security?
7) Do you find yourself worrying and stressed out when trying to fall asleep at night?
8) What will it take for you to let go and let God be God in this area your life?

<u>**Prayer 2 Pray Today**</u>:

Heavenly Father,

Please forgive me for not trusting you to provide for me. Forgive me for putting more faith in a job, my spouse or my parents than I have in you to supply my needs. Forgive me Lord for allowing money to control my life, my decisions, my emotions and my attitude.

Help me to give thanks and be filled with your joy despite what I have in my purse/pocket/bank account. Help me Lord God to not let lack or abundance change who I am, or how I behave towards others. Your word tells me that the cattle on a thousand hills belong to you, and that if I seek first your Kingdom, everything I need will be added unto me. Your word promises me that in you I have sufficiency in ALL things and that I lack nothing. Your word says that if I have faith the size of grain of mustard seed, I can speak to the mountain be thou removed and cast into the sea and it shall be moved; that nothing shall be impossible unto me. So, Lord I speak to this lack in my finances, this problem in my marriage, this disease in my body, this trouble in my life and this confusion in my mind commanding it to be cancelled, uprooted and destroyed in Jesus' name.

Now Lord, I know you are no respecter of persons and that what you did for Jacq and Rob you are willing and able to do for me. I need to witness a financial miracle in my life Lord God and today I put my trust and faith in You to receive my Divine financial breakthrough. I will be careful to give you all the glory and praise for the blessings you entrust me with. I will be your mouthpiece and tell of your goodness so that others can be drawn unto you.

I thank you for giving me the very air I breathe and for letting it be a constant reminder of your ability to provide every single thing I need to survive in this world. Thank you for knowing what those needs are long before I even ask and when I do, I thank you Lord for doing exceedingly and abundantly above and beyond all that I've even asked for. I thank you in advance Lord for supplying ALL of my needs according to your riches in glory. These things I pray believing, receiving and counting them as done in the mighty name of your son Jesus Christ.

Amen.

CHAPTER 4

Now Faith … Yes, Please!

"Now faith is the substance of things hoped for, the evidence of things not seen." **Hebrews 11:1**

You can *Breakthru2Transition* by turning your eyes away from your ability towards God's ability. This type of life-changing shift comes with great reward for those who are willing to take its mandatory leap and dare to walk by faith. It marks the beginning of real freedom and purposeful living.

Here's the problem though… most of us are accustomed to reacting according to what we 'see' and have been conditioned into believing that's all there is; because we believe what we 'see', we speak and act accordingly. However, God's word instructs us to place very little credibility in those things which we can see, but rather focus our mind (spiritual eyes) on things unseen. Many have eyes (natural sight) but cannot see (spiritually).

Whenever you look with your natural eyes at your situation and circumstances, you forfeit your ability to access Divine intervention and supernatural assistance (favor, deliverance, healing and provision). Likewise, this distorted viewpoint causes you to <u>not</u> seek His wisdom, to <u>not</u> live in faith and to <u>not</u> trust in His word. Essentially, trusting in the limited views emanating from your own eyes is the perfect way to miss out on God's best. What you can see determines what you will get…see abundance, see His provision and His promises.

> **Say 2 Self:** Don't be wise in my own eyes or convinced by what I see. Remember to look through my eyes of faith.

We learn in **Hebrews 11:6**, that without faith, it is impossible to please God, and it greatly displeases Him when we lack child-like humility, trust and confidence in Him.

It is also written in **Hebrews 10:38** that *"The just shall live by faith, but if any man drawback, My soul shall have no pleasure in him."* Who are 'the just' the Bible is speaking of? The just are His born-again children who are *righteous* in His sight, i.e., you and me.

Please allow me to make it plain for you. Take a quick look around your home, office, out of your window or into a mirror, if you will. What do you see? Chances are you see something you can touch, smell, hear or taste. In other words, they are tangible items like objects, fixtures, people or animals, right? Okay.

Now, let me ask you a question: Is what we see, taste, touch, hear and smell all there is? Of course not.

The very air we breathe cannot be seen. The soundwaves which allow us to hear cannot be seen.

Most importantly, the spiritual realm where evil unclean

spirits reign is unseen:

Peace, joy, contentment and love are all unseen.

The Holy Spirit which comforts us and leads us into all

truths … cannot be seen. The (positive or negative)

emotional energy generated by people when you are in

their presence is unseen, but it can certainly be felt.

What's my point here?

I want you to know and understand that there's more to

this life than we will ever fully comprehend or behold with

our natural eyes. The most amazing things are seen with

spiritual vision – eyes of faith. Faith has no limits. It is not

to be compromised by any situation or circumstance;

neither should you.

Say to Self: Faith is my most powerful creative force, it pleases God and makes the impossible possible in my life.

Faith is the substance, the evidence of what you are *A*sking,

*B*elieving, *C*rying-out, *D*epending-on and *E*xpecting God

to do in your life. It is the stuff your dreams are realized by,

the conduit for miracles and the catalyst of change in any

area.

In fact, The Law of Attraction and The Secret were

both spawned from God's Faith Laws, so if your thoughts,

words and actions are functions of faith, He honors your

belief, and desires are manifested in your life. One of my

favorite verses about faith is **Hebrews 11:29** and it

reads: *By faith the people passed through the Red Sea as on*

dry land; but when the Egyptians tried to do so, they were

drowned. What I absolutely love about this verse is that

God allowed His people to do the impossible, yet when the

others tried to do the same, they were consumed.

My Lord!!

Say 2 Self: My faith activates the hand of God and manifests all that He desires for me.

Faith gives us access, abilities and a supernatural advantage that is remarkably and indescribably mind-blowing. By faith God is invited onto the scene to do amazing things on our behalf. And guess what? The size of your faith does not matter to God. You don't even have to have a large amount.

> *"For truly I say to you, if you have faith the size of a mustard seed, you will say to this mountain, "Move from here to there," and it will move; and nothing will be impossible to you."* **Matthew 17:20**.

Do you know how small a mustard seed is? Well, it's a good 50% smaller than a poppy seed or a clove and measures about 1 to 2 millimeters (0.039 to 0.079 inches) in diameter. Let's just say … teeny tiny, itsy bitsy. So, don't spend **NOT 1 MORE DAY** thinking or believing that you don't have enough faith! God is not concerned with the amount of faith you have, because He is the one doing the work, making a way, and answering your prayers.

Know This: The bigger the obstacle, sickness or trial, the bigger your God will move on your behalf, and your little mustard seed of faith in Him - in yourself - makes it all possible. Your faith is simply the remote key which unlocks His power and grants Him access to perform great things in your life. Hold on to it. Keep the faith!

> **My Faith Formula:** My problem(s) + God + a little faith = mighty miracles, signs & wonders

I'm sure just like me, you've met people who have suffered and survived some incredibly difficult times, and I bet you too marveled at the tremendous amount of faith they exuded to make it to the other side of their situation. Yet, when you commend them for having had such great faith, they humbly say that they don't have any more faith than anyone else, or that they had no idea how much faith they possessed until that event. Either way, there's no question in their minds that without God, they couldn't have made it …period.

Nevertheless, there comes a time in every believer's life when our little mustard seeds of faith appear weak in the face of life-threatening health issues, insurmountable debt, generational curses, constant family conflicts, unexpected financial crises or recurring relationship disappointments. In those trying times, purposefully reactivate, supercharge and ignite your faith by the words you choose to speak in the midst of the storm.

***Speak those things that be not as though they were* (already manifested)** *Say what you desire to 'see' manifest through eyes of faith, NOT that which is visible with your natural eyes.* Say what ought to be and what you want to see (abundance, healing, unity, peace, provision and resolution). Stop speaking words which reinforce the calamity at hand or callforth hurt, harm and danger onto the scene of your circumstances.

Example: "They probably won't hire me." "I guess it's going to be another one of those days where everything that can go wrong for me will." "Oh girl, I feel like I'm coming down with the flu."

To speak what you see when the storms of life are raging will invoke fear, give validity to its reality and the endless possibilities of what could go wrong, what might not work and what is likely to happen next. These words and emotions are enemies of faith and work vehemently against you every time. Guard your mouth gate; watch carefully over your words because therein lies the power of life and death. Determine **NOT 1 MORE DAY** to speak words of lack, defeat, sickness or doubt!

Say 2 Self: I must only speak words that agree with the word of God and align with what I want. Otherwise, I cancel and disallow the very things that I desire.

UNLESS you take the limits off of yourself by speaking words of faith, your words will both reflect and reproduce whatever you perceive which limits you in the spirit realm! It is imperative to keep your mind on the things that *cannot be seen*, so that you will be able to intentionally speak, command and call into existence that which you desire.

Fear Facts

A mind full of fear is far from sound … it is diseased, paranoid, anxiety riddled and unable to function in the face of tragedy or life challenges. False Evidence Appearing **R**eal (**FEAR**) is one of the most destructive tools of the enemy. It immobilizes the spirit, attacks the soul, paralyzes the mind and wreaks havoc on the body. "God has not given us a spirit of fear but one of power, love and a sound mind." – **2 Timothy 1:7**

FEAR: Focus Equals Absolute Reality – even though it's *false evidence*, it has your *FOCUS.*

Say 2 Self: What I focus on becomes my reality. Faith or Fear … the one I feed grows stronger in me.

This is what makes fear feel and seem so *real* … it consumes your vision … it prevents your ability to focus. Fear has kept many brilliantly gifted and talented people from reaching their God-given potential and achieving their dreams.

Beware of fear and its deceptively unsettling ability to annihilate your confidence and obliterate your **TAGs**, particularly *if* your focus is not on something bigger than yourself. Know that **(FEAR)** the very thing the enemy intends to use to knock you out of the game is often an indicator of a God Move in the making – your clue that He is up to something awesome and that your miracle is on the way.

This ugly spirit of fear, regardless of form, must be cast down, resisted and rebuked out of your mind daily by the word of God. Speaking words of faith, based upon the promises of God, gives you power over **ALL** the power of the enemy … especially fear.

Be on the lookout for the fear of failure, fear of success, fear of other people's opinions and the fear of death, which are four of the most gripping fears you will regularly have to fight against. Know that <u>none of these are from God</u> and are designed to keep you from living your best life now. Pause here and boldly evict the spirit of fear from your life.

> **Say 2 Self:** God is my refuge, my strength, my defense, my protector, my healer and my redeemer. The Greater One lives in me; I have no fear of what man can do/say.

You don't have to be deceived or defeated **NOT 1 More Day** by this cruel wile of the enemy in Jesus' name.

Therefore, you must use your words as weapons of mass destruction whenever fearful thoughts bombard your mind and skew your focus. Otherwise, you run the risk of succumbing to it and having your dreams, hopes and potential swept away by its vicious undercurrents …

never rising to your true greatness.   At least you may have until this very moment, I decree and declare that fear will no longer have dominion over your mind, and in the mighty name of Jesus **NOT 1 MORE DAY** of tormenting thoughts will be able to hinder you. From this day forth you will begin to speak words of faith over your situations boldly, according to the power that worketh in you, and you will be steadfast, unmovable as you abound in the work of the Lord.

Say 2 Self: My words impact my emotions and solidify my beliefs; those beliefs govern my behavior!

Consider these words from Rosa Parks,

"I learned to put my trust in God and to see Him as my strength. Long ago I set my mind to be a free person and not to give in to fear. I always felt that it was my right to defend myself if I could. I have learned over the years that when one's mind is made up, this diminishes fear; knowing what must be done does away with fear."

Just like God's plan for Rosa, His plans for you are astonishing, and His vision for your life is filled with excitement and abundance. Your dreams, goals and passions are connected to His Divine vision and present a huge threat to the kingdom of darkness. You are His light!

Remember darkness hates the light, but don't be afraid to shine. Shine brighter and represent your Heavenly Father.

See the biggest best picture for your life. Dream BIG!

If your dream doesn't seem impossible or make you uncomfortable, guess what? It not big enough. It's gotta be BIG to motivate you and activate the God in you.

Small dreams are wishes lacking the faith and power required to propel you forward and bring glory to Him!

Sure, you may be somewhat unclear of the outcome, unsure of the right timing and feel a bit unprepared for the journey, but when your will is aligned with God's purpose for your life, He assumes responsibility for the outcome.

If He ordains a thing, He will sustain it. If He brings you to it, He will get you through it. He will give you what you need. He will provide the right resources and the right people to assist you. Trust His heart when you can't trace His hand, and know that by faith, He will be with you every step of the way.

Whenever you are faced with anxiety or fear of the unknown but have a burning desire for change and believe this desire is of God, *stop – look – and listen*. **Stop** and ask for God's guidance, then **look** *for signs of His movement* and *listen* with expectancy for Him to clarify the vision.

Be patient. Be still. Silence the fear, ask for wisdom and hold on to your faith in His word, His promises and ability.

I love what He promises here …

> **Jeremiah 3:33** *"Call to me and I will answer you and tell you great and unsearchable things you do not know."*

He further promises to …

Psalm 32:8 *"I will instruct you and teach you in the way you should go; I will counsel you and watch over you."*

But wait, He's not done promising!

Proverbs 3:5-6 *"Trust in the Lord with all of your heart and lean NOT unto your own understanding; in ALL of your ways acknowledge Him, and He will direct your path."*

What if you aren't convinced that He will speak to you, or perhaps you aren't sure how to recognize His voice? No worries, you belong to Him … His sheep know His voice. He knows exactly how to Divinely orchestrate everyday situations and circumstances to speak on His behalf in ways that will give you the all of the necessary confirmation you need to proceed.

Fret not thyself, He knows how to meet you exactly where you are!

Often, I've turned on the TV and flipped to a random channel where the Gospel was being preached, and the preacher's message spoke directly to me.

On numerous other occasions, I've scrolled through Facebook and landed on an inspirational post or podcast that confirmed what was uncertain in my spirit. I've turned on the radio, flipped stations and He'll have a song playing that ministers to my heart/soul. At sundry other times, God has allowed someone to call, text or even used a stranger to approach me with a word of wisdom or a prophetic message.

Likewise, I've been the stranger that He's instructed to console, encourage, meet a need or provide an answer for someone else. I can even recall several nights of falling asleep wondering and trying to figure out a situation when God gave me a word in my dreams. Trust me - His ways are limitless - He speaks using various means. Listen for His still small voice. Expect for Him to send you a word. Without a shadow of a doubt, I assure you that He can, and He will. God's got your back! Trust Him.

> *"And I will bring the blind by a way that they knew not; I will lead them in paths that they have not known: I will make darkness light before them, and crooked things straight. These things will I do unto them, and not forsake them."* **Isaiah 42:16**

He will order your steps when you decide to walk in close communion with Him and commit to His purpose for your life. It delights Him to give you the desires of your heart.

He wants nothing less than His best for you, knowing this makes me cringe when unlearned people talk about God's Children living *'above their means'* … scripturally **He IS** the Believer's *'means'*! Jesus died to grant us abundance.

> *"The thief comes only to steal and kill and destroy, but I have come that they may have life and have it to the full."* **John 10:10**

Abundant provisions - **Psalm 132:15**

Abundant blessings - **2 Corinthians 9:8**

Abundant wisdom and knowledge - **Isaiah 33:6**

Abundant fruit and food - **Daniel 4:21**

Abundant love - **2 Corinthians 2:4**

Our needs are met according to HIS riches in glory NOT ours. God knows no lack; abundance **IS** His way. Don't fear living an abundantly blessed life. Carry on!

<u>**Questions to Ponder:**</u>

1) What is your greatest fear?

2) What would you do differently if you truly believed that God had your back?

3) List three things you would be able to do right now if you were free from the grips of fear?

4) What will it take for you to let go of your fears and begin trusting God?

5) Can you remember the last time you decided to step out of your comfort zone and trust God? What happened?

<u>**Prayer 2 Pray Today:**</u>

Lord God thank you for not giving me a spirit of fear but one of power, love and a sound mind. Thank you for sending this rhema word today to deliver me from the bondage of fear which has kept me from living my life to the fullest. In Jesus' name I bind and rebuke any conditioning, faulty thinking and deceptive trickery the enemy may try to keep me from fully trusting you God. I ask you Father to replace any doubt, fear, unbelief and negative thoughts with those of faith, courage and boldness. And Lord, should I become weak in my faith, send forth your laborers unto me with a word of hope and restoration.

Build me up on the inside, hide your word in my heart so that I might not sin against you and deliver me Lord God from the deceptive voices of those living in darkness. I know that faith cometh by hearing and hearing by the word of God, so give me a hunger and thirst for your word. Help me to seek you while you may be found.

Thank you for equipping me to walk boldly in the direction you have purposed for me. Thank you for helping me refocus and transform my mind with your word as I look to you for guidance and protection. I thank you Lord, that no weapon formed against me shall prosper because you are with me. Thank you for being for me which is more powerful than even the whole world being against me. Thank you for the blood of Jesus which covers me and shields me from all hurt, harm and danger.

*In Your Son Jesus' mighty name, the name above all names, I declare victory over self-defeating thoughts and agree to live **NOT 1 MORE DAY** as a captive in the prison of fearfulness. Father, I thank you for my renewed ability to walk by faith, favor and forgiveness into the abundant life you have planned for me.*

Amen.

CHAPTER 5

TAG You're It

> *"Our deepest fear is not that we are inadequate. Our deepest fear is that we are powerful beyond measure. It is our light, not our darkness, that most frightens us. Your playing small does not serve the world. There is nothing enlightened about shrinking so that other people won't feel insecure around you. We are all meant to shine as children do. It's not just in some of us; it is in everyone. And as we let our own lights shine, we unconsciously give others permission to do the same. As we are liberated from our own fear, our presence automatically liberates others."* **Marianne Williamson**

Have you ever wondered how it is, and why it is, that some people are able to live their dreams while many others can't seem to get over the many humps n' bumps in life? Some have work that they love and enjoy which happens to both pay and serve them extremely well financially, socially and emotionally. This 'work' allows them to live a blessed and balanced life with seemingly minimal stress and anxiety. Yet there are others, such as I was, who toil day after day – barely making ends meet, mentally, physically and emotionally drained, struggling to keep it all together –

who only experience nominal joys and marginal pleasures from day to day and year to year. What is the difference in these two distinctly different life experiences? How is this possible? Is God a respecter of persons? Has He gifted some and not others? Does He bless some and curse others. Not at all. Scripture assures in **Matthew 5:45** *God causes the rain to fall on the just and the unjust alike*. Keep in mind that back in biblical days, rain was a great blessing because of the agricultural era and the dependence on the income from each harvest, rain meant life. Some considered presence of it to represent the presence of God.

So again, what is the difference that makes the difference from one person to the next? Our answer lies in an individual's propensity to (**RACE**) **R**ecognize, **A**ctivate, **C**ommit to and **E**mploy their **TAGs** (Talents, Abilities and Gifts).

Recognize Your TAGs

In the first chapters of this book, I shared with you the importance of knowing and understanding what your **TAGs** were and determining how God intended for you to let your light shine using them. He created you to be self-sufficient when you were born because He'd deliberately placed **TAGs** in you. Allow the thought of coming into the world as a newborn with something on the inside of you that predestined <u>you</u> for greatness. OMG, how powerful is that?!

At birth, you already possessed what Denis Waitley refers to as the *seeds of greatness*!

These seeds only need was to be watered, nurtured and developed by parents, universal teachers, life experiences, and God Himself as you grew in years.

Then, at the appointed time, you and the **TAGs** would become one; you would suddenly be awakened and brought into the full awareness of your Divine purpose.

Recognizing what you were born, created and destined to do, or become, is the key to unlocking fulfillment, joy and prosperity in every single area of your life. Recognition of your God-given **TAGs** is crucial to your success. If you still are unsure, keep reflecting and keep seeking God. He will reveal the gift He's bestowed upon you … if you ask Him. As you continue reading, and as you go about your daily routine – remember to *LISTEN*:

"Whoever is of God hears the words of God. The reason why you do not hear them is that you are not of God." **John 8:37**

"I will instruct you and teach you in the way you should go; I will counsel you with my eye upon you." **Psalm 32:8**

"When the Spirit of truth comes, he will guide you into all the truth, for he will not speak on his own authority, but whatever he hears he will speak, and he will declare to you the things that are to come." **John 16:13**

"He who has ears, let him hear." **Matthew 13:9**

<u>Activate Your TAGs</u>

> *"Every morning you have two choices: continue to* sleep *with your dreams or wake up and chase them." --* **Carmelo Anthony**

When we receive a new credit card in the mail, regardless of the credit line we've been granted, it must be activated. If we fail to follow the required steps for card activation, we can never expect to benefit from having the extended lines of credit. So, yes, you were born with a specific set of **TAGs** ... fully loaded, waiting for their presentation to the world; to avail you to an abundant life, but it must be activated. Can you see the wasted potential, and what a disgrace to the giver that would be in both instances?

Don't be satisfied with merely possessing a gift, having others acknowledge your talent or applaud your abilities. Get up, get going and make some tangible life changing transactions with what God has given.

To further demonstrate how to activate your **TAGs**, I'll use what is referred to in the world of education as a non-example: Imagine that until today, you have simply been following a script that perhaps your lineage has written for you. For generations, most of the people in your family, valued higher education, may have all chosen a certain profession or field of interest and have impressed upon you that you too should follow suit … *so you do.*

On the other hand, you may have been born into a cycle of poverty and lack of formal education, where the need to survive was the main focus and you were taught to hustle hard, fight for what you want and make ends meet by any means necessary … *so you do.* In either scenario, your **TAGs** are not given any consideration, and by following the established patterns - succumbing to circumstances prevails over all.

Because most children strive to please their parents and the societal masses by walking in generational footsteps, they frequently forego their own dreams and desires just to keep the peace. While cantering around in their adult bodies, their choices often appeal to outwardly imposed goals and forced financial, social, familial demands. Rather than charting their own course and swimming against the tide, they die quietly within. Walking and living dead lives yet trying to look alive they struggle. [**TAGs deactivated**].

This **TAG** annihilation frequently results in one of two plights – acquiescing to the progression of the family profession or lying in state at a family procession – without ever tapping into purpose or utilizing the gifts within.

Or, let's look at the flip side of this coin. You know your **TAGs** and have an insatiable desire to pursue them further. You would love for them to define you and become the essence of your life's work. Your passion is strong.

Your knowledge is vast, and your opportunities are endless, yet someone whose opinion is important to you does not endorse your choices. Instead of being true to yourself, your **TAGs** and your dream, you conform to their perspective and dissolve your passion. [**TAGs deactivated**]

The moment you renounce the gift, dim your light and lessen your shine, you are automatically enrolled into the army of mediocrity. **[Dream deferred]** Whenever you deny your gift to appease, 'fit in', not call attention to yourself, or to just live an 'ordinary' life … expect to be tormented by a myriad of dis-eased days and restless nights.

> **Say 2 Self:** My TAGs will not allow my purpose to stop calling until I answer!

NOT 1 MORE DAY was written for the dis-eased and restless among us. Those who are ready to answer the call.

So how do you activate your **TAGs** and walk in your light?

You become one with it. You allow it to lead you. You follow it. You share it. You use it. You shine!

Dare to trust and fully believe that what's inside of you is worth fighting for and has the potential to change the lives of someone else for the better… especially YOU!

> *"As good stewards of the manifold of grace God has given you, each of you should use whatever gift you have received to serve one another."*
> *1 Peter 4:10*

Activate your **TAGs** by grabbing hold to the belief that what you have to say, share or do on this earth is important.

> *"… But each man has his own gift from God; one has this gift the other has that."* *1 Corinthians 7:7*
>
> *"There are different gifts, but the same spirit."* *1 Corinthians 12:4*

Your desire plus your faith-inspired fearless actions are your **TAG's** activation code … you've got to want what God has for you badly. Bad enough to break every chain of complacency and mediocrity – bad enough to break

through every generational curse against you - bad enough

to break free from every thought of inferiority and

insecurity.

You must fight for your vision and use your **TAGs** to

catapult every area of your life to the next level.

Back in the days of MLM (multi-level marketing) when

I attended a plethora of motivational meetings, inspirational

seminars and emotionally laden events with leaders from

all over the country, I noticed something. One common

recurring theme in every single story shared was a burning

desire to overcome obstacles life had placed in the way.

Success blockers like situational and generational poverty,

addictions, low self-confidence, health challenges, and fear

threatened their attainment of personally defined goals.

Those hinderances to time/money/social freedom were

conquered by a hunger and thirst passionately called their 'WHY'.

It was so exciting to hear testimony after testimony of people who looked just like you and me, share how they made it to the top ranks against all odds and despite the crappy cards they'd been dealt along the way.

Each victor had a 'WHY' and stressed how crucial that 'WHY' was in keeping them from giving up or giving in when the going got tough. When people doubted their vision and when the situations/circumstances of life were less than kind, their "WHY" provided the energy to keep pushing on.

My dear friend, a wealthy Vietnamese businesswoman shared her powerful story with me, and I'd like to share it with you. At the tender age of 16, my friend's mother told her that the only way she would have a decent shot at a better life was to come to the United States, the very land that many of us who were born here take for granted. Filled with far more desire than fear, she was taken to a small boat and left by her impoverished family to journey alone...alone into the big, new world that awaited her.

In the dark cold bow and stern of the boat, she lay curled and cramped up with a host of strangers, who like her, were determined passengers. Together, they journeyed like sardines in a can for four long weeks.

Twenty-eight hot days and dark desperate nights where food, water, and basic hygiene items were scarce. When the boat finally arrived in the US, after what seemed an eternity, she couldn't walk. She was too weak. So frail. Her body locked and ached from the many lonesome and frightening hours, she traveled in the tightly bent and squashed position. Determination and desire were the lifeblood that kept her alive until she was met by foster parents at the dock who nurtured her back to health.

Once nursed and nurtured back to health, her education began. She studied hard, with the belief that a good education had the ability to change her life. Although she missed her family dearly, she was thankful for a chance at something better than the lifestyle her native land could offer. Knowing there was nothing to go back to and that she had to make the most of this God-given opportunity … she persevered in hope laced with the sweetest vision of someday having her loved ones living here too.

Graduating with an engineering degree and being blessed with a high-paying job at a Fortune 500 company several years after her arrival, she began to rescue the family she'd courageously left behind. One by one, she brought them to the US to experience and share in a quality of life unlike anything they could have ever imagined. Yes, because of one faith-filled sixteen-year-old who risked her very life to venture a far with only a dream of entering the promised land of opportunity, her entire family was blessed with abundance. Her 'why' was "gi-normous." Her vision was clear, and her noble intent aligned with God's vision for her people brought her dream to life.

I encourage you to discover your 'why', activate your **TAGs** and make the decision to fritter away **NOT 1 MORE DAY** living beneath your God-given ability. You don't have to settle. You don't have to fear, but you do have to stir up the gift inside and get busy working on your dream to make the rest of your years the very best of your years.

You cannot afford to sit on the sidelines of your life **NOT 1 MORE DAY**; *"You are the light of the world. A city on a hill cannot be hidden."* **(Matthew 5:14)** Someone somewhere is depending on the winner in you to come forth. Someone needs your shining light to rescue them from a life of darkness!

<u>Commit to Your **TAGs**</u>

I remember well over twenty plus years ago, visiting Braeswood Assembly of God where the infamous Nicky Cruz (a gang leader turned evangelist) was speaking, and while listening to his incredible testimony, God spoke to me for the first time. Sitting there, amid a packed congregation, I was flushed from head to toe with an indescribable warmth accompanied by a full body chill - simultaneously.

Although I'd heard a friend, or two, say that God had spoken to them, it had never happened to me.

He said, ***"Don't let what you don't have keep you from getting what I have for you."*** His words were liberating, yet they had absolutely nothing to do with Nicky's message. I wrote them down quickly inside the front cover of my Bible for safekeeping and my own evidence that I'd heard God.

No longer listening to Nicky, I kept looking at what God spoke to me. I read it over - and over - and over again in awe that Almighty God, Himself, had spoken to me. ***"Don't let what you don't have keep you from getting what I have for you."*** The feeling was surreal, yet what He said has continued to unshackle me when faced with the dim reality of my own limitations. His words still ignite my faith; give me the much-needed confidence to pursue my every desire.

The most obvious example of my putting God's words into action, happened back in 2006 while searching for the perfect home for my seventy-eight year old father and me.

According to my credit and income, the homes I visited were in the $110,000-140,000 range. My uncle William, also a real estate broker, and I selected a nice home within 'my means', but God had other plans. The new home buyer agent suggested that I become a realtor based on my personality and demeanor which was music to my uncle's ears. "I told you!" He reinforced. My open-mindedness made considering their input so much so that when I left the builder's model office, I processed the idea.

Before going to my apartment, I stopped by my dry cleaners. The owner's wife had just given birth to a baby girl, and I sent her some shea butter by him as a gift a few weeks prior. Now this shea butter balm, just one of the many pampering products in my Warm Spirit MLM line, reportedly removed stretchmarks. When I arrived, I couldn't wait to ask him how she and the baby were doing and find out how well the butter was living up to its reputation.

He said great to both and asked how my business was going. I told him good, but that I would be taking real estate classes soon to sell larger ticket items like houses. He did not hesitate to tell me that he would be my first client. Jaw dropped, I asked – "So you want to buy a house?" "No, I will need to sell a house." He corrected. "Ok, so you guys are planning on moving then?" I presumptuously asked. "No, we don't live in the house. It is empty. In fact, its been empty for five years, but it will sell fast because it's beautiful and has two master bedrooms – one up/one down." He explained.

Mind you, this was exactly what my daddy and I needed … two master bedrooms. My God! "How perfect would that be?!" I thought while asking him where it was located and how much they were interested in selling it for. "Well we bought it for $185,000 in 2001, but it's worth at least $195-205,000 now. Just let me know when you're done with your classes and ready to see it." He offered.

It sounded perfect, but I mean, it was more than fifty thousand dollars over my budget. I shared my desire to purchase a home for daddy and me. He invited us to go see the house and possibly buy it. (LOL right)

My inner dialogue raced, "Ok God, this sounds like a Divine set up - big time! You know I can't afford a house like that, and if I see it I'm going to want it. This ain't right." Before I could hear anything from God, the dry cleaner asked, "So, when do you want to go look at it?" Although I knew I couldn't afford it and didn't want to waste his time, I did want to see the floorplan and checkout the neighborhood. We agreed on a day and time.

The curb appeal was breathtaking! From the cul-de-sac lot, light beige brick, manicured lawn and quiet streets, I became excited. Once inside I high vaulted ceilings, dual master bedrooms with private baths, ceramic floor tiles and a jacuzzi garden tub greeted me. Talk about everything I loved plus a ton of lovely custom features, this was it.

RAL (reason and logic) weren't at all impressed, "Girl get your butt up outta here, and tell these folks thank you. You already know you can't 'do nothing' with this house." My faith however, thought otherwise: I knew God _could_ bless me with a home like that, I just wasn't sure He _would_. During battle between the two (my faith/RAL), the Holy

Spirit quickened me about what God had spoken to me years prior: ***"Don't let what you don't have keep you from getting what I have for you."***

I didn't have excellent credit. I certainly didn't have a six-figure income. However, based on what He'd told me I knew, if He wanted this incredible adobe for daddy and me, it would be mine. Well, you can best believe He made it happen in a most creative way! I tell you from the day I moved in until 11 ½ years later, when a historical flood wreaked havoc on our city and caused my Divine relocation to the other side of town, I loved every square foot.

That home was nothing short of a sheer delight, peaceful dwelling place and testimony of God's goodness to my family, my friends and me. Proudly I shared my story with every visitor who entered through the doors, giving Him all due glory, honor and praise. Won't He do it?!

Somebody in your immediate proximity is looking at you, watching your life and your struggle to get inspiration. In need of hope and a glimpse of God's movement in the life of a 'believer'- they suffer. They need to see a modern-day miracle. They need to witness you busting a faith move - to see you committed to a dream, vision or idea that's larger than you – to see you rise above the troubles blocking your way. Trust and believe that the eyes upon you are many. Suffering in the silence of their own pseudo-safety zone, they look and listen desperately to hear an encouraging word from you. Will you be God's spokesperson? His witness?

Our world today is ravenous for a manifestation of God's provision, promises and protection. Aimlessly many search – for an up-close example to follow – a shining light to lead the way to a better life. Beloved, you are that light. Your shine can brighten up their darkened spirits and change their situation, but you must be willing to tell your story. Unashamedly, with passion and commitment it's time to let your life speak for the Kingdom. Share your testimony!

> *"Light yourself on fire with passion, and people will come from miles to watch you burn."* - **John Wesley**

You must walk by faith to do *that which* is beyond your means, *that which* is out of your reach, *that which* causes you to swim against economic and social tides; *that which* you know will require God's help. And when you allow your purpose – your dream – your desire for something greater - to pull you out of the known into the unknown … rest assured that others will show up. Some will show up as helpers to assist you along the way.

Some will show up as spiritual supporters to cheer you onward. Some will show up as companions to join you on your Divine destiny's journey. Some will show up as witnesses just to watch you blaze the trail which they are too afraid to tread. Of course, a few haters and naysayers will surface too. You will recognize them by these words: *"If I were you … you probably shouldn't … I know somebody who … what if … have you thought about … remember the last time … did you pray on this?"*

Stay focused, keep the faith in the midst of the whispering doubting Thomas' and trust God to do what you can't. Know that there are more people rooting for you than there are ill-wishers … hold your head up, lift your eyes up and get ready to ascend by grace to the next level of you.

Remember that you have the promise of God:

> *"Therefore, my dear brothers and sisters, stand firm. Let nothing move you. Always give yourselves fully to the work of the Lord, because you know that your labor in the Lord is not in vain."* **1 Corinthians 15:58**

Let God use you as His vessel. Be His ambassador and expose others to His limitless ability to bless, heal, set free and deliver. He will equip you to fulfill His purpose, complete His assignments and overcome every obstacle along the way. Resist the urge to worry over every detail.

He has the plans already mapped out … trust Him - you will not - you CANNOT fail. You've got this because God's got you!

"Call to me and I will answer you and will tell you great and hidden things that you have not known." **Jerimiah 3:33**

"And whatever you ask in prayer, you will receive, if you have faith." **Matthew 21:22**

Employ Your TAGs

"I must work the works of him that sent me, while it is day: the night cometh, when no man can work." **John 9:4 KJV**

Once you have recognized, activated and committed to your **TAGs** the last thing to do is put them to work. The world will tell you that if you don't use it you will lose it, but the Bible says that the gifts and calling of God are irrevocable; He won't take them back. **(Romans 11:29)** Isn't that good news?! I'm so glad that His ways are not our ways and that His thoughts are not like ours, because I know several folks who will take back what they give you if you don't make use of it within 'their expected' timeframe.

We serve a patient and merciful God who understands our human dilemmas, downfalls and distractions. He knows that the enemy is very crafty at keeping us from focusing on our purpose by keeping us *busy*.

A lovely Christian counselor once helped me get on with the business of employing my **TAGs** when she asked me to explain my daily routine. At that moment my list included work, Facebook, an online home design game and that was it. No exercise. No regular prayer times. No writing. No reading. No hubby date nights. Nothing but work and meaningless, idle fillers had made up my days for years – no wonder I was feeling depressed, disconnected and drained. Some way, somehow, I had become so used to following the script that I just stopped living. I was barely even present. Walking, talking and working dead. But God!!!

Her question flipped on a light within in me; I was awakened. My eyes and spirit lit up. I wanted to jump up from my seat, run around the building and scream, "Yes, I got you now devil … I see where you've been winning. Clearly, my daily routine was a flat line. Game over. Thank you, Jesus!!!"

The dark cloud looming over my head disappeared instantly, and I could see my light again. Remembering my **TAGs**, crystalized my purpose … *I'm a writer, I'm a* *coach, a teacher and a natural motivator (always have been and always will be).*

Suddenly snapped out of idle living, God's ambassador of change for living abundantly (AKA Mizjaq) returned to my proper purposeful place. I immediately deleted the design game and limited my FB time to less than an hour. Hubby night and prayer time was set; my writing took flight; I became a certified Life & Vision Board Coach and began coaching local teachers of writing. Now regarding the physical exercise implementation part (lol) … well, we're not quite there yet.

Seriously though, the amount of time I'd wasted doing absolutely nothing that had anything to do with my **TAGs** astounded me. I'm talking about some staggering numbers of years vanished … gone like a puff of smoke.

One day while busily arranging my new home office, I ran across a DBA I'd gotten in 2008 for **HTM3 Solutions** – my company name – which was set to expire in August of

2018. Where had the years gone? I was devastated. Ask me what I had done with the business in the nine years since assuming its name … not much at all! I ordered business cards, set up an email, and signed up with Leisure Learning to conduct a few sessions in 2012 but when only 3 people enrolled, I cancelled the classes. In retrospect, that was a missed opportunity big-time because once again, my **TAG**s were unemployed, I dangerously burned through years like wildfires raging in California.

Can you relate? Have you wasted time doing so much of nothing that little evidence exists to distinguish one year from the next in your life? If so, your AHA moment may have just smacked you in the face too. Good, now let's go! It's high time to boldly evict your distractions and give them **NOT 1 MORE DAY** to occupy your **TAGs** place.

You may not have all the specifics, finances or plans laid out, and that's ok. By simply shifting your attention, making a commitment to pursue your purpose, activating your **TAGs**, understanding the truth about your significance and your relationship with the world around you, amazing opportunities and people are soon to show up in your life just as they have in mine.

Know that when your light is shining … it draws and attracts like 'lights.' Hence, the Law of Attraction in full effect – what you energetically exude, you bring about because your thoughts and feelings directly affect the outcomes, experiences and chain of events taking place on your behalf. God, your Father, has given you a gift rich in its ability to bless to you abundantly as you share it with others.

Proverbs 18:16, promises that your 'gift' will make room for you and bring you before great men.

This is your season of breakthrough. Your season for grace and favor abounds! It's your season to take back the time, joy, energy and expectations the enemy has stolen;

your season to reconnect with your purpose, re-envision your vision and realize your dreams. With God, there's no such thing as too late. He can rewind the clock and redeem the time if you are ready to trust Him.

Say 2 Self: God's timing in my life is always perfect because He is not limited by it! He's an on-time God.

<u>Questions to Ponder:</u>

1. How are you spending your God-given time?

2. How many dreams have you put on the back burner? Why?

3. What do you need to do to get on purpose?

4. What has hindered you in the past from pursuing your dreams, goals and heart's desires?

5. Who and what has the enemy been stealing time from in your life?

<u>Prayer 2 Pray Today:</u>

Dear Heavenly Father,

Thank you for your loving patience towards me. Thank you for this awakening and for helping me identify where the locust, cankerworms and enemy have been robbing me of my time and energy. Thank You Lord God for restoring unto me the joy of my salvation and the vision you have given me for my life.

Lord, I ask in Jesus' name for you to forgive me for the times I've personally wasted by being afraid of what others would think or say. Forgive me for not believing in myself and for doubting the inherent greatness that you placed in me when I was created in Your Image.

Father I thank you for opening my eyes of understanding so that I can begin to see through the eyes of faith and my ears so that I can hear your voice without distraction. Lord please let me not be diverted, deceived or delayed any longer from your perfect will for my life. I invite you to use me as your vessel, as your beacon of light and hope for those in darkness. Help me to let my life's light shine before men so that they may see my good works and glorify You in Heaven.

Father send laborers across my path to assist me along this journey and give me the discernment to know who is of You and who is of the enemy. Let their fruits be known and their hearts' intentions be crystal clear to me. Please guard my mind and my spirit from any negative influences as I begin to walk by faith. These things I pray believing I have already received in the powerful name of Your Son Jesus Christ.

Amen.

<h1 style="text-align:center"><u>CHAPTER 6</u></h1>

Take Control and F-L-Y (First Love Yourself)!

> *"Love the Lord your God with all your heart and with all your soul and with all your mind and with all your strength ... love your neighbor as yourself."* **Mark 12:30-31**

There are four distinct types of love in the Bible: <u>Storge</u> – familial love between parents and children, brothers and sisters, you know the kinfolk sort of love. Then there is <u>Philia</u>- the love of mankind, human to human, the compassionate and wholesome caring for the well-being of one another. Throughout scripture it is made apparent that the very essence of God is love, and <u>Philia</u> is the kind of love Christians are expected to display. Since God Himself is love, the amazing love He has for us is immeasurable, unconditional, sacrificial and pure. We call the God kind of love <u>Agape</u> - the Greatest love of all. However, the last of the four types is <u>Eros</u> – the romantic, physically attractive, sexually oriented, erotic kind of love that God solely purposed for marriage.

According to my experience, **<u>Eros</u>** gets us in the biggest trouble, and if we are not careful, has the greatest potential for damaging and distorting our love of self. More about that in my next book. Wait for it! □

The truth of this matter is that far too many times, I have been guilty of loving others <u>MORE</u> than I've loved myself. I am certain that I have plenty of company, but why is that?

Why do we (*especially women*) exert so much energy, expend so much time and exhaust ourselves to the point of no return loving folks who aren't even remotely interested in or capable of loving us back?

Why ya'll?

Why is it so hard to love ourselves as the Bible instructs us to do? Where did we get off track thinking that everything and everyone we love comes before us; that we are to serve, satisfy and sacrifice until we can't no 'mo' …

that's not biblical my Sistah saints. God has given clear

instructions:

"Love your neighbor <u>as you love yourself</u>." Mark 12:31

Seemingly somehow, our *identity*, in our minds, rests in our

ability to love, give and do for others what we don't take

time to love, give and do for ourselves. But I get it, we are

born nurturers, cultivators and creators, gifted with the

power to carry an egg from its conception for nine months

to birth, turn a house into a home, and transform raw

ingredients into delectable culinary masterpieces. So, with

these things in our genetic profiles, we approach

relationships with an open heart (a blank canvas if you will)

which is ready to take the least bit of attention or affection

and turn it into a lifelong union ... a sheer work of art.

In fact, by the time we finally tire from – pouring into

one bottomless pit after another - nursing everyone's

wounds while we bleed profusely - accommodating

everyone's needs but neglecting our own, and making sure

that anyone connected to us is well nourished emotionally although we starve for significance, we are as used up as a wrung-out dishrag. There is no energy, spunk or reserve left for us.

The idea of self-love is a controversial one, yet a point worth clarifying before we move forward. There are undoubtedly two ways to 'love yourself': one is based on arrogant conceited pride which the Bible flat out warns against, and the other is established upon **(Agape love)** knowing that God loves you which is exactly that which allows you to love your neighbor as yourself with **(Philia love).**

When you truly fall in **(Philia)** love with yourself, in the manner He intended, you become more accepting of others, more appreciative of your own individuality, and more deliberate about the decisions you make. Every thought, word and deed can now become rooted in love … because you finally **(Philia)** love you enough to make wholesome choices. In the absence of self-love, choices are reckless and costly; your mind, body and soul end up paying a hefty toll.

Awareness of Self-Love: Growing up as an only child, I always wanted siblings and someone with whom to share my lot of toys, games and goodies, but God decided to allow His choice of brothers and sisters to show up later in my life. Longing for *someone to play with* kept me unable to embrace the gift of 'me' I'd been given. This 'lonely only' plight, caused me to settle in a variety of ways. However, after a multiplicity of surface encounters, one-sided relationships and draining conversations with toxic people, I learned that all company wasn't good company.

One day, the realization hit me … there was nothing wrong with taking myself out to lunch/dinner and that it was okay to go out of town or to a movie alone. So, I did. Surprisingly, I enjoyed my own company and discovered how easy and uncomplicated it was to just spend time with me. In so doing, I vowed to look outside of myself for love **NOT 1 MORE DAY**. I was set free … God loved me, I loved me, and for once that was enough.

I recall a cruise, taken a short while ago, where my goal for booking it was quite simply to relax, exhale and enjoy. Period! Any sightseeing, overdrinking and partaking in the robust schedule of onboard activities was optional at best. Desperately seeking a respite from an assortment of physical, mental and social demands, I packed my bags and for the first time … my laptop. On this much needed voyage, intentionality led me to overlook the daily 'Fun Times' agenda, and consciously check in with myself to see what I *really* wanted to do.

Having cruised an embarrassing number of times in the past, I knew all of the happenings (deck plans, menus, shows, games, destinations) oh too well. Although I was extremely grateful for such privileged familiarity, and my newly garnered Platinum VIFP status, this trip made it even more obvious that it was time to expand my nautical portfolio.

There were still so many different ports to visit, people of other cultures to see and exciting fun activities to explore.

With that consciousness in the horizon of my mind, once we docked in Key West, Florida, I decided to forego trekking off ship and stayed behind to partake of the quiet enjoyable hiatus onboard … when most of my fellow cruisers were venturing off at port. How many times did I need to simply visit Key West for a slice of pie?

Sitting on the Lido deck, taking pleasure in the cool breeze and sharing the solitude of seaside serenity with about 20-25 other guests, felt sinfully blissful. Stolen moments like this reinforced just how much I enjoyed spending time with me as my handmade, tobacco-colored, wooden window seat offered the most incredible view of the deep ocean blue canvas sprinkled with sailboats, jet skis and the elite island life it surrounded.

Aromatic smells from a variety of hot freshly baked pizza, spicy Mongolian fare, and delicious Guy's burgers bombarded my nostrils while crew members walked by dangling tempting specialty drinks. A low buzz of busy workers scurried around in preparation and in anticipation of the thousands who were expected back aboard after-shore excursions, shopping sprees and adventurous Key West tours. In between the breathtaking views, incredible aromas and snippets of paradise, using reflective strokes on the keyboard of my laptop - I made my 'me-time' stand still.

On several past sailings, I'd heard a few say that they frequently choose not to disembark at select ports, in exchange for taking advantage of uncrowded shops, empty pools, discounted spa treatments and select onboard in-port events. Of course, at that time, I thought, "How crazy is that … you spend money on a cruise and don't get off at port? Yeah, right whatever!" Now, I marvel at such wisdom.

To take the concept of 'me-time' even further, listen up. I promise you are in for a treat. ⏺ My mother and I decided to celebrate my 53rd birthday nautically and booked a 14-day Carnival Journey Southern Caribbean cruise to the Cayman Islands, Aruba, Barbados, Dominica, Grenada, St. Marteen and Curacao. Talk about an amazing two-week adventure at sea … I strongly recommend that you try it at least once if you haven't already.

But what was beyond awe-inspiring for me during this adventure was the large number of boldly independent and interesting women we met on the ship who were traveling solo. They knew no one, and they were confidently traveling abroad alone. Talk about 'doing you'…these ladies had mastered the art of loving themselves and were living their best lives abundantly as a result. Our many conversations, ever so rich and refreshing as we sailed from port to port, reeked of a freedom I'd never imagined.

Wow, talk about freedom?! Talk about confidence?! What greater expression of self-love could there be than to set sail for two-weeks? I've been enlightened by their shine.

Acquisition of Self-acceptance: As one voluptuously-endowed female from birth, I must admit enjoying a decent self-image. *Tiny in the waist and cute in the face* described me perfectly, even though by the age of 18 yrs. old, each thigh (28 inches) was larger than my 26-inch waist, I was still considered a brick house. Then my biggest challenge was the gap in the back of my blue jeans which had to be taken in to properly fit my well-defined waist, yet still allow enough room for me to squeeze hips and thighs into.

However, it wasn't long before time, hormonal imbalances and a sedentary lifestyle, brought about drastic changes to my physique, putting an end to my slammin' figure.

What was once bit-sized boobies were somehow converted into DDs. The former flat stomach pooched, inflated and drooped like an oversized beach ball on hydraulics. And, there was little left to distinguish the back of me from the front.

Yep, it happened.

I went to sleep one night, woke up one day, and voila there I was … forty and overweight. Still cute in the face, but twice the size in the waist, I decided to work with what I had. My mother used to always say, "Accentuate the positive and eliminate the negative." Maxing out at almost 375 pounds at one point, I held my head up and strutted ALL my stuff … some days the strut took more effort and energy than others, yet I pranced on.

One humid hot Houston summer's day, I received a call from a dear sister-friend who had been involved in a near-fatal car accident.

We talked as she lay in Ben Taub Hospital with cuts all over her body, a crushed pelvic bone, and a dislocated hip crying hysterically because she'd been told she would never walk or have children again.

I emphatically and confidently informed her that the devil was a liar and went on to explain how the doctor's report was not her final answer. I told her she had a choice and asked her whose report she would believe, theirs or God's. "You will walk again and have more children in Jesus' name. God has plans for your life that's why you are still here. You've got to know that. He's got you!" Her trembling voice pierced my heart, "Sister, I don't want anyone to see me like this, but I need you." I knew she did. Fear gripped her. She was traumatized – but God!

As I was getting ready to go visit and pray with her, the enemy started messing with me. Nothing I put on looked right. Nothing fit right. Outfit after outfit was tossed on the bed and on the floor as I searched for this 'fat day' attire. Finally, out of total exhaustion, sweat and frustration, so that the 'fat day' wouldn't get the best of me, I settled on a pair of stretched light blue Capri pants and a tropical, cotton, cap-sleeved top. Passing by the last mirror on the wall as I walked toward the garage door, I shook my head in disgust. My arms looked huge and this stomach … "Eww, how repulsive. Look at you," the enemy whispered. "Whatever, get behind me Satan!" I scarfed back. Despite his fiery darts and tormenting, I jumped in the car and headed to the hospital fully armed with my blessed oil and Bible.

Sweating and walking down what felt like a mile-long sidewalk, several patients were sitting in various spots almost strategically positioned along my path. The first was an older gray-headed gentleman with an amputated leg sitting on a bench. I looked at him and smiled. He spoke and said, "Hello Beautiful, how are you today?"

Well you already know I was in my feelings from the fleshly clothes battle I'd just fought at home. "I'm good and you?" I responded. "I'm blessed to be here, praise God!" he proudly exclaimed. Wiping the sweat from my brow, trying to ignore the huge lump I felt in my throat, I kept walking. About ten steps ahead, I saw a young lady about my age, sitting in a wheelchair with one arm … smiling and looking directly at me as I neared. "Hi, how are you doing today?" I asked. "I'm blessed and highly favored of the Lord my Sistah!" she boasted.

I felt faint … this weird feeling from my head to my feet almost overtook me. Just as I attempted to regain composure and enter the main lobby doors, there was a lady being pushed outside in her wheelchair about to go home. I nodded my head at her and smiled – stepping aside for her to be rolled past.

She looked up with brightest glow in her eyes and said, "I'm going home today, God is good. By the way, I like your outfit. Have a blessed day!" I mustered up a "Thank you. Yes, He is … you too." Oh, my Lord, I was beyond done. And to seal the deal, the Holy Spirit spoke to me and said, "Anyone of the people you have seen today would love to have your body right now. They have been greatly afflicted and are more appreciative than you, yet you have both arms, both legs and good health."

By now tears were streaming down my face. I had been convicted like a first-degree felon on the day of sentencing. I rushed to the nearest restroom and cried profusely apologizing to God for being so ungrateful for my health and well-being. He was so right! There I was with limbs intact and walking around healthy, yet I'd been complaining and moaning earlier because my body didn't look like it used to.

Instantaneously, I decided to accept me just as I was. Humbly I asked God to forgive my ingratitude and promised Him I'd never forget how fearfully and wonderfully made He'd created me. From that day until now, **NOT 1 MORE DAY** has been spent in brutal combat with self-criticism or internal grumblin' and mumblin' about my physical state.

I know for a fact many of you are struggling with some aspect of your body you wish looked differently. When you turn on the television or log onto social media, image after image speaks to that part of you which you'd gladly swap out if you could. Or how many of you find yourselves comparing <u>how you look now</u> to <u>how you used look</u> back in the day; to someone you think is more attractive than you?

The enemy uses these **SDTs** (self-defeating thoughts) to destroy your self-esteem and infest you with self-loathing. Your self-talk becomes unkind as you look in the mirror. Secret shame and inferiority creep in and there you have it – you are now a helpless victim of your own undoing.

My Sistah, recognize who it is that hates you and that he doesn't want you to love who God has created you to be. Understand the danger in succumbing to this part of his scheme which is to keep you from letting your light shine and reaching your God-given potential. But God! I decree and declare that you were uniquely created in the image of a perfect God who loves you just as you are. You are beautiful in His sight. You are His. Regardless of your height, weight, skin color, facial features, hair type or physical challenges, you are just right – right now.

You are worthy of much love, respect and joy. Accept who you are today! See yourself as God sees you … with eyes of love and adoration. Promise to spend **NOT 1**

MORE DAY comparing, belittling, berating or browbeating yourself. Become your own BFF … you deserve all of you!

<u>Arriving at Self-forgiveness:</u> Here's a newsflash for you - you're human - you've made mistakes so what? The shocking truth is we all have. Get over it. Sounds a little harsh, huh? Well, I'm sorry. (LOL) No, not sorry.

I mean it … get over what you would-a, could-a, should-a done differently. Stay present in the present - keep moving.

Whatever happened way back when and back then, happened. Whatever didn't happen, didn't happen. Okay, you missed some opportunities, messed up a couple of times and said yes when no was the obvious answer. Maybe you kissed a few frogs and took in too many dogs in your quest for love. It happens to the best of us. Grow and move on.

Count it all joy. You learn better to do better. You've been taught some valuable life lessons, and believe it or not, all the craziness you've been through is the very foundation upon which the amazing woman you are today stands.

Yes, girlfriend you ARE amazing if for no other reason than you survived what should have taken you out. So, go ahead and say thank you. Thank those who used you, tried to abuse you and who didn't have any intention of loving you. They were not for you … they were just teachers in the classroom of your life. Take the lesson, know better and be better as a result.

I know things happened, stuff hurt; don't let that hinder or haunt you. Keep your head up. Keep believing in you. Don't waste your essence in bitterness or time and energy trying to get even. Don't wallow in your poop … it will only stick 'n stink. Don't look back – snap back – get back to doing you. Master the message that was masked in the madness and move on.

Here's some great news: unlike most people we know, God doesn't rub your nose in your mess or remind you repeatedly about what you did wrong. He forgives and forgets when you admit your shortcomings and wrongdoing to Him. What this means is that God is bigger than your faux pas. He loves you despite your desire to live your way instead of His way, aka your *sin nature.*

The Bible says that if we *confess* our sins, God is faithful and just to forgive us and cleanse us from all *unrighteousness.* What is sin? Sin is missing the mark, failing to do/not do a certain thing, thereby functioning against/below God's standard for living. How do we *confess our sins?* Acknowledging that we messed up, asking God for the strength and wisdom to get it right, is true confessing. But don't stop with the confession … repent. Turn away.

Once you know better, act on that knowledge and hold yourself accountable for doing that which is right in the sight of God. I must add here that we can put on a good front, straight face and holy walk before others, but we can't fool God. He sees and knows our every thought/deed. Strive to remain true to Him not man; live a life pleasing in His eyes and watch abundant blessings spring forth in every area.

> **Say 2 Self:** I will seek God and His righteousness by trying my best to live according to His word and will.

Let's consider the parable about the woman who was caught in the act of adultery. She was brought before Jesus by those who found her cheating. They expected Him to shame her with judgment, but Jesus told them that anyone who was without sin could throw the first stone.

Obviously, she had been caught in her sin. She was guilty, and according to the laws of her day, she should have been stoned to death. Yet, one by one, everyone in the condemning crowd turned away and fled the scene. How so?

Not one of them was without sin. Not one of them was qualified to condemn her. Jesus looked up at the woman and said:

> *"Woman where art thou accusers ... Neither do I condemn you. Go and sin no more."*
> **John 8:3–11**

Why did this woman's accusers tuck tail and run? Yep, you got it. They were just as unclean, just as guilty of falling short in some area, but how many of you know it's easier to point out the faults of others than to focus on your own? The point Jesus made is clear: they ALL had sinned in some shape form or fashion which meant none of them was fit spiritually enough to punish the adulterous woman.

The problem remains today just as it was then, that some misinformed folks think sin comes in sizes … you know small, medium, large and extra-large doses. One sin is greater than the another. Most are quick to point fingers at someone else's faults while failing to consider their own.

Many of these same people notoriously lie, steal, fornicate and cheat but frown upon anyone with a LGBQT lifestyle justifying the disdain because their sinful acts are somehow more serious. Wrong. Sin is sin.

Who are we to judge and rank trespasses? God is the only judge. **1 John 5:17** tells us that ALL wrongdoing is sin, but not every sin leads to death.

Many of you reading this right now, have attempted to punish and crucify yourselves for choices and decisions you've made in the past. For years, you have beat yourselves up and needlessly suffered from self-inflicted wounds because YOU refuse to *love* YOU enough to *forgive* YOU.

----- **STOP** -----

This self-badgering is not of God. Whatever it was that you did at that time, you either did it because you felt it was best for you, felt good to you, simply what you wanted to do or you didn't know better. Whichever the case may be … it's over now, done, and behind you. Realize this and release yourself. grown from your mistake(s). **Let them go.**

You don't need to remind yourself, doubt your ability or question your integrity **NOT 1 MORE DAY!** Stay woke my friend. Don't let the things you did/said yesterday keep you from living a joyful and victorious life today. You must believe that you deserve a second, a third and possibly a fourth chance to get it right. God is a merciful God. If He is willing to forgive you … who are you to keep yourself down and bound?

Look in the mirror – look in your eyes and tell yourself, *"I love you, and I forgive you. I promise you that* **NOT 1 MORE DAY** *will I blame you, curse you or be angry at you for the choices we made in the past. We are in this together; this thing ain't over. It's a new day. God is on our side, and we will win!"*

> *"Do not call to mind the former things; pay no attention to the things of old. Behold, I am about to do something new; even now it is coming. Do you not see it? Indeed, I will make a way in the wilderness and streams in the desert."*
> **Isaiah 43:18-19**

> *"If we confess our sins, he is faithful and just to forgive us* our *sins, and to cleanse us from all unrighteousness."*
> **1 John 1:9**

Questions to Ponder:

1. Have you been beating yourself up and feeling ashamed about something you've done?

2. Are you willing to ask God for His forgiveness and turn away from your sin?

3. Are you willing to forgive yourself?

4. Have you been over judgmental of others and wanted to see them punished for what they may have done to you?

5. Are you ready to be freed from your guilt, shame and harbored resentment?

---

5 Step Soul Healing

a) Make a list of all mistakes you've made
b) Ask God to forgive you
c) Ask Him to help you forgive yourself
d) Burn or rip that paper into shreds
e) Declare your freedom from the past

Say 2 Self: Today I give myself permission to live fully and freely. I now deserve the best because I've been forgiven and set free by God.

<u>**Prayer 2 Pray Today:**</u>

Dear Heavenly Father,

I come to you asking for Your forgiveness and for You to cleanse me from all unrighteousness. There are many things that I have willingly and knowingly done that were against your commandments and perfect plan for my life. There are others that I did not know were sinful. Lord, please forgive me for both.

Forgive me for being wise in my own eyes, for leaning unto my own understanding and for allowing the desires of my flesh, the lusts of my eyes and my foolish pride to get in the way of righteous living. Forgive me for the decisions I made in the past to get even with others, to do my own thing and to have my own way knowing that what I was doing was displeasing to you. Forgive me for any angry, jealous, bitter or evil thoughts I may have held against my trespassers. Lord God, please forgive me for the words I've spoken against You, Your word, Your people and Your commandments to justify my actions.

In Jesus' name deliver me from that familiar rebellious and stubborn spirit which rises up against me whenever I attempt to do what's right. Help me be controlled by Your Holy Spirit rather than my flesh. Help me develop a strong desire to do Your will and convict me when my thoughts drift into waywardness. Protect my idle mind and fill it with pure, loving and wholesome thoughts, so that the desires of my flesh, and the temptation of sin, will not triumph over me.

*I speak victory over my mind, body and spirit in these areas, and by the power of my words, I decree and declare that **NOT 1 MORE DAY** will I allow sin to dominate my life. In Jesus' name I pray.*

Amen.

CHAPTER 7

What You See Is What Shows Up!

"If you don't have a vision you are going to be stuck in what you know, and the only thing you know is what you've already seen." **Iyanla Vanzant**

Trying out a new masseuse is not one of my favorite pastimes since I've had the same amazing hands massaging my body for the last 10 years. He's so incredibly relaxing and systematic that I've followed him to several locations, transferred my membership twice and have him on speed dial to do in-home sessions from time to time. Nevertheless, to avoid driving across town, every once in a blue moon I venture off to a spa nearby. Well today my adventure produced more favorable results than most. Mike was a friendly young Asian with shorter hands and fingers than I was accustomed to, but they were strong. The energy in our 2-hour session was upbeat and positive … we clicked. His specialty – deep tissue – did not interest me in the least; his assignment was to put me to sleep. He failed.

Anyway, conversation flowed from family values to American abundance to relationships to this question: "So, Mrs. Green what attracts women to men? Like what attracted you to your husband?" **<u>Internal Dialogue</u>:** *Great, not only is this guy a deep tissue guru; he is attempting to have a deep dialogue with me while I'm trying to drift off into LaLa Land. Well, it ain't happening today I see. Ugggh!* "Well Mike, I'd have to say his level of self-confidence." Mike thought that was the coolest answer. "Wow!" he exclaimed. "That's something I don't have," he said. *Huh?!*

I almost jumped up from the table in shock. "What?! Why not?" I asked. He told me that when he was younger, he was a pudgy little fellow and remained that way until a few years ago. He dropped over 80 pounds and changed his eating habits. Now let me just add in here that the dude was ripped – I mean he looked like a man who eats, sleeps and breathes inside a gym.

I couldn't imagine him having low self-confidence. "Mike, are you kidding me? Man, you are a nice looking, well-built guy. You are buff! What's up?" I asked in amazement. "Mrs. Green, I don't see myself like that … I still see me pudgy." He ashamedly confessed. OMG! Revelation, inspiration and clarification combusted in my head.

> **Say 2 Self:** <u>What</u> I 'see' becomes my reality, and <u>how</u> I 'see' myself determines the quality of my life.

That is the power of your vision – your ability to 'see.' It will make you or break you in every single area of your life. Or at least it would have until today because the secret is out. You've got to 'see' yourself as you want to be NOT as you *are* right now or as you *were* back then.

The way you choose to 'see' yourself has a tremendous impact on what shows up and dictates how you experience/interact with the world around you. Look through your eyes of faith, and 'see' what God sees for you!

Mike and I are at opposite ends of the spectrum regarding what we 'see' when we look in the mirror. Instead of seeing the excess weight as I carry it now, I still 'see' the *cute-in-the face-tiny-in-the-waist* voluptuous Diva I was twenty-five years ago. Baby please. That's where the enemy has slyly deceived me into celebrating a positive self-image and a healthy self-esteem while the delusion is fast at work keeping me obese. But you already know what I'm about to say … I refuse to not 'see' myself **NOT 1 MORE DAY** as the woman I used to be. I will be who God intends me to be.

In choosing to 'see' the truth, I must first acknowledge and reverse the effects of what a sedentary lifestyle, a fast food addiction and backwards 'seeing' has done to me. I can then choose to 'see' a healthier, lighter and more energetic version of me because that's who I <u>intend</u> to become. Now, I am fully able to affirm that choice by confessing a desire to live and not die in denial of what obesity looks, feels and destroys like. I will intentionally set my intentions to win!

The final step in transforming what I "see" into who and what I desire to 'be' is putting my words and faith in motion. Literally! I'm sure you've heard that faith without works is dead right? Meaning, you can believe a thing all day – all night, but without acting on what you believe, you are just wishing and dreaming in vain. Put a date, a plan and a clearly focused intentionality in place with that belief then bust a move in faith.

Faith Move Formula
My vision + My belief + My actions = Amazing results

What I've shared with you here is how your 'seeing' is directly responsible for your 'being', and that when you can 'see' the truth, you are empowered to live freely in that awareness. Mike and I were both negatively affected, in different ways, by the same backwards 'seeing'. His made him unjustly <u>less</u> confident, and mine kept me unjustifiably over poised. Both are equally paralyzing.

'Seeing' yourself as you are right now, although it may indeed seem like your reality, does not have the right to remain your reality moving forward, unless you desire it to be so. Choose right now to not to miss 'seeing' who you are destined to become **NOT 1 MORE DAY**.

Refuse to 'see' yourself in any way other than how God sees you, and to not 'see' your life's glass as half-full instead of almost empty **NOT 1 MORE DAY**. 'See' it abundantly, 'see' it complete and seize it as yours. Speak it. **Let it be so**!

My prayer at this point in your reading is that you are obtaining some clarity and identifying some stinking thinking (**SDTs**: *self-defeating thoughts*) which contributed to your present reality: mentally, physically, emotionally and spiritually. I declare that you will begin feeling somewhat hyped, pumped up and excited with a new burst of energy stirring up inside. My prayer is that you start to see the potential lying dormant within you all this time awaiting your awakening.

Allow the words on these pages serve as your personal wakeup call … your best self is ready to get up! If you're desirous of change but feeling a somewhat unprepared to make it happen right now, that's ok … I got you. Let's just pause to embrace and truly imagine the possibilities of breaking free – living free – enjoying life. Walk with me.

As children we could pretend and 'play-act' effortlessly. Without any limitations, conditions or reservations, we could *freely be* whomever we *wanted to be.* Think back to how you played as a child. Take me for an example, I had big plans for a grand life and picked the late great Michael Jackson for my hubby. ☺ Y'all, that's right! I was married to Michael Jackson from the age of 7 until about 11, and we had four children: two girls Michelle/Mya and two boys Michael/M'Jon who was named after my father John. My best friend, who lived across the street and would spend sun up to sun down at my house playing with me, was married to Marlon which made us sister-in-laws. Lol. I'm telling you, we spent innumerous days, months and years as these glamorous celebrity wives who cooked, shopped and lived in the mega mansions we created in my garage. No one could convince us otherwise. We were indeed Jackson wives.

Okay, do you get my drift with this imagination thing now? Good, come on - let's activate your imagination. Close your eyes and envision yourself totally free from what you've been 'seeing' day to day. Now yourself permission to imagine with no limitations or rules. How does it feel?

Let's go a step further with a few guiding questions:

What do you want to <u>see</u> happening in your life right now? What do you want to <u>do</u>? Who do you want to <u>be</u>? Where do you want to <u>go</u>? What legacy would you like to <u>leave</u> behind?

Take a mental picture of the exact life, job, mate, relationship or physique you've long imagined, in other words, 'see' it! Now think about your **TAGs** – think about where you shine. Think about your strengths. Think about what you would do if you knew you could not fail.

Imagine doing *that* very thing that you enjoy and do so effortlessly for a living … getting paid to do what used to seem, and still seems, so natural and fun. Get a clear vision. Set your intentions, and then **write the vision** as God instructs in **Habakkuk 2:2**. Make it as descriptive and detailed as you can. Designate a special tablet, journal or make electronic notes in the Cloud … just be sure to compose your vision. **'See it'. Write it. Date it.**

Put it where you can see it regularly. Allow it to compel you – keep you committed in the face of tests, trials and tribulations. If you really want to kick it up a notch, make a vision board with pictures, images and power words depicting all that you have imagined for each area of your life. Create one for your career, relationship, personal, financial and spiritual goals. These will propel you forward and serve as a focused reminder of your innermost desires and soul purpose. The magic will begin to happen, I promise!

> "Create the highest grandest vision for your life because what you believe is what you become." **Oprah Winfrey**

Every moment of every day, you have the autonomy to decide how to address many facets of life. Generally, you approach these pieces of life's puzzle either from a <u>realm</u> of possibility or from a <u>place</u> of *'pessimisity'*. The difference between a realm and a place is this, one stems from a supernatural Kingdom mindset and the other from a fleshly common mindset. And based on the lens (spiritual or carnal), used to view ourselves, our lives, our individual

circumstances and interactions with world in which we

live, we speak words that perpetuate that perspective.

This perspective determines how that which is physically

seen, is 'seen' by one's inner being.

Just think for a moment about the familiar glass half-full or

half-empty example. The amount of water in the two

glasses is visibly the same, yet how it is perceived dictates

how it is 'seen'. How it is 'seen' dictates what is spoken or

said about it, and you already know how much creative

power your words possess.

Hence, I argue against the catchy statement: "It is what

it is." Hmmm. Is *it* really **what** *it* is, or **how** we 'see' *it*?

The truth lies in the **Book of Genesis 1:1-31**

> *"In the beginning God created the Heavens and the earth. The earth was formless and void, and darkness was over the surface of the deep, and the Spirit of God was moving over the surface of the waters."*

As God's Spirit moved, He had a vision … He 'saw' something more. ***Then God said,*** *"Let there be light";* ***and there was*** *light.* Notice what God saw physically was a huge void filled with darkness, but because of His vision, He spoke a command to call forth and produce light.

He 'saw' spiritually into existence and spoke it into physical form. Let's try it again. Water covered the earth and that's all there was until God had a vision … He 'saw' something else.

*Then God said, "**Let there be** an expanse in the midst of the waters, and **let it** separate the waters from the waters." God made the expanse and separated the waters which were below the expanse from the waters which were above the expanse;* ***and it was so.*** *God called the expanse Heaven.*

Pay attention to the slight difference in what happened here – this time, He made (created) the vision He 'saw'.

Are you with me?

Ok, how about one more very detailed example of His vision?

*Then God said, "**Let there be** lights in the expanse of the heavens to separate the day from the night and **let them be** for signs and for seasons and for days and years; and **let them be** for lights in the expanse of the heavens to give light on the earth"; **and it was so.***

God 'saw', God said, and it was so! Now, I ask you again, after reading this do you believe in life when things happen **it is <u>what</u>** it is, or is it a result of <u>**how**</u> we 'see' it?

I invite you to pause and absorb the powerful Story of Creation to 'see' (no pun intended) how everything in the earth was spoken into reality by God.

Whenever He spoke the words **let there be** to those things He *saw*; they were instantly transformed into what He desired to 'see'. How marvelous and magnanimous is this amazing 6-day account of the power of 'seeing' and speaking words intentionally?!

The Story of Creation excites me immensely because I know that God made us in His Image. He has given us the same creative power to effect change in our lives as well as in the lives of others. You don't have to be limited, bound, overwhelmed or feel helpless **NOT 1 MORE DAY** … 'see' what you desire, speak **<u>let there be</u>**, and it shall be so in Jesus' name. Can I get a 'Thank you Lord' right here?

> **Say 2 Self**: I manifest what I 'see' when I speak words of faith to my surroundings, circumstances and situations.

Here's the promise:

> *"For verily I say unto you, That whosoever shall say unto this mountain, Be thou removed, and be thou cast into the sea; and shall not doubt in his heart, but shall believe that those things which he saith shall come to pass; he shall have whatsoever he saith."* **Mark 11:23**

Because of this promise, we have the authority and ability to speak what we 'see', and have it manifest in our lives. Yes, you've got the power right now in your mouth to change your world. You were created in His Image to emulate what He did, but He doesn't want you to stop there … there's so much more!

During Jesus' time on earth, He performed many miracles ranging from healing the sick to raising the dead; He left us with yet another promise …

> *"Most assuredly, I say to you, he who believes in Me, the WORKS that I do he will do also; and GREATER WORKS than these will he do, because I go to My Father."* **John 14:12**

I sense the enemy trying to mix signals here, so let me clarify … NO, you are not God or Jesus, **BUT** you have been given the authority and a sound promise to do what they did. **If** you dare trust and belief the word as it is given.

However, that my Beloved is the main stipulation – you must believe what you are saying when you speak and trust God for the outcome. Point blank period … That's it!

It's not your duty or responsibility to figure out the details of who, when, where or how it will happen …

simply trust and believe that it can. The details are God's

business; He uses our faith in Him to do the impossible.

God is not a man that He should lie; if He has made a

promise in His word you can best believe He will make

good on it. Put His word and His ability to the test with

your unwavering faith, trust and total dependence on Him.

Become childlike in your belief – take the limits off

yourself and your God. He specializes in impossibilities.

When lenders reject you, friends turn their backs on you,

family forsakes you, your bank account is negative, your

strength is failing, and the doctors have given up on you …

celebrate. You are in the perfect position for a miraculous

and mighty move of God. When all you have left is your

faith in Him you are on your way to elevation and victory.

Hold onto your faith no matter what and resist the urge to

doubt. Doubting deeply offends your Heavenly Father

because He alone is worthy of your complete trust, yet many of you would rather rely on yourself or someone else instead of your Creator. It's a huge slap in the face of His unconditional love, mercy and ability to provide, protect, defend and deliver on your behalf. He is The Good Shepherd and you are His sheep. Hands down, He has your very best interest, best future and best moments on hold waiting for your faith to activate the manifestation.

Alright I get it, when you feel like time is of the essence and your back is against the wall, trusting God gets difficult. You want to fix whatever is broken or handle whatever has gotten out of line yourself, but my Dearest, you can't. Here's where you have to let patience have her perfect work – here's where you will be tried in the fire – here is where if you didn't have this book, you would be tempted to throw in the towel and lose hope. But God!

During these pressing (depressing/oppressing) times, you will keep your sanity and your faith in tow by speaking God's word to yourself and your situation. I mean speak them like mantras … like every time anxiety, worry, doubt and fear creep in run them out of your mind with what He has promised. Use His word to quench darts of defeatism.

You are invited in **Isaiah 62:6** to put God in remembrance of His word when you pray and to keep reminding Him until the promises are fulfilled. Here are just a few of the many, many life-changing promises found in His word:

God, you said, I am blessed and cannot be cursed. (Numbers 23:20)

God, you said, Your Favor is not for a season, but for a lifetime. (Ps 30:5)

God, you said, whatever I touch I will succeed. (Proverb 3:6)

God, you said, if I decree a thing, it will be established for me. (Job 22:28)

God, you said, You would prosper me even in a desert (2Chronicles 20:20)

God, you said, You said the seed of the Righteous is blessed (Genesis 17:18)

God, you said, my children will be mighty in the land (Psalm 112:2)

God, you said, You would give me beauty for ashes (Isaiah 61:3)

God, you said, the moment I pray the battle will turn (Dan.9:23)

God, you said, I am more than a conqueror (Romans 8:37)

Now let's talk it out: *"**God, you said (scripture)** and God, you promised to **(scripture)** so Father I thank you in advance that **(confirm the promise)** because I know you are faithful and can be depended upon to do just what you said."*

My dear friends, I assure you not based on what I have heard, read or been told – I know firsthand that God honors HIS word! When you speak His word in faith back to Him, it will not return unto void!

> *"For as the rain and the snow come down from heaven and do not return there but water the earth, making it bring forth and sprout, giving seed to the sower and bread to the eater, So will My word be which goes forth from My mouth; It will not return to Me empty, without accomplishing what I desire, And without succeeding in the matter for which I sent it."* **Isaiah 55:10-11**

Now there lived a certain man in the Bible days with a son who was bound by a mute spirit which caused him to be thrown to the ground with horrible seizures and foaming at the mouth. The child suffered for years as a result, so his father approached Jesus' disciples to have it casted out. Unfortunately, because they lacked sufficient faith to do so, despite having witnessed many afflicted beings cured by Jesus in their presence, they could not. Jesus instructed the father to bring Him the child. Jesus said unto him …

> *"If you can believe; ALL things are possible to him that believes."* Immediately the father of the child cried out and said with tears, *"Lord, I believe; help my unbelief!"* **Mark 9:23-24**

My sole purpose for writing **NOT 1 MORE DAY** was to strengthen your faith, evict your unbelief and empower you to transform your life from lack to abundance in every area. I pray these Holy Ghost directed words of mine will become yours and ignite a fire within you so bright that your light will not flicker. You will rise-up and change your world and the world of those around you.

Check out this quote, which by the way, I absolutely L-O-V-E by Millionaire Steve Jobs:

> *"Here's to the crazy ones. The misfits. The rebels. The troublemakers. The round pegs in the square holes. The ones who see things differently. They're not fond of rules. And they have no respect for the status quo. You can quote them, disagree with them, glorify or vilify them. About the only thing you can't do is ignore them. Because they change things. They push The Human Race forward. And while some may see them as the crazy ones, we see genius. Because the people who are crazy enough to think they can change the world, are the ones who do."*

SSI: Soul Self-Inventory

1. Is what you 'see' impossible for you to do alone?
2. Write a reflection about what resonated with you in this chapter most.

CHAPTER 8

A Faith Move In Motion

So okay, go ahead and color me 'crazy' as I continue to prove my status as such. My dream car used to be a Mercedes … any model, any color or any series. I didn't discriminate. I simply drooled over them and often thought the owners were the most fortunate folks on the planet. Where did this deep admiration come from? Well just sit back, relax and let me take you on a fascinating faith-building journey:

Growing up, my Daddy was affectionately referred to by many as the George Jefferson of Houston. He owned seven dry cleaners and always wore the finest of tailored suits wherever he went. Think of how my favorite TV host, Steve Harvey, dresses today and you've got the perfect picture. I never once saw my Daddy in 'regular clothes' like jeans, jogging suits or t-shirts. Quite a classic man, he carried himself in the most distinguished manner

… even when lounging at home, recreating outdoors or piddling around in the yard.

In fact, he even used to cut our grass, in hot humid Houston weather, wearing a pair of outdated suit pants with an old dress shirt hanging out over them - cuffs rolled up to his elbows - and sporting an old beat up pair of black leather loafers. Daddy was such a class act, he would pay me weekly to iron his pajamas, boxers and handkerchiefs.

On Saturdays, starting at age 14ish, he paid me a nice salary to work with him all day. I would enjoy servicing the front counter of our dry cleaners in 3rd Ward: greeting customers, checking in stinky clothes, working the cash register and counting money at the end of the day. Mind you this particular location was open 24 hours a day, near downtown, which meant at times the clientele consisted of a robust milieu of people from every nationality, socio-economic status and profession. Teachers, doctors and blue-collar workers just to name a few, were our regulars.

Not surprisingly, I most fondly remember Black Sam, a real live NicNic silk shirt, flared wide legged pant, heavy gold chain wearing pimp. He held the number one spot as our best-smelling, smoothest talking, largest-cleaning-bill-having and highest tipping customers. You can best believe anytime he showed up, every female employee working the front counter rushed to assist him. Unless of course I happened to be on duty, at which time these doting ladies kindly let me takeover (per his request).

Black Sam got a big kick out of having 'Lil Ms. Miller' wait on him, and I surely didn't mind receiving the nice twenty-dollar tip he was infamous for giving. So, let me tell you what had happened on this most impressionable day. Looking out of the window, I noticed that Black Sam didn't pull up in either of his usual shiny long Brougham Cadillac Devilles (*he had two - candy apple red metallic with white leather seats and a shiny bright gold one - both with personalized license plates*).

He rolled up in a brand-new seafoam green Mercedes Benz 500 Sedan and parked it right next to Daddy's long black and white, customized, Cartier Edition Lincoln Continental Town Car. Focused intently on the ray of sunlight beaming down on that glistening Mercedes Benz grill, I stood jaw dropped. What in the world kinda ride was that?! Hypnotization took over as my eyes slowly caressed the curves of the 500 sedan's body, each piece of chromed out silver trim and the shimming Armor All dripping from the big Michelin tires. I was beyond done! From that day on – my head did 360's whenever I saw a "Big Body Benz" of any color on the road. To me, it was and still is, the king of the road.

Eventually blessed to get my first car at fifteen, a red two-door Ford Granada, my own vehicular history began. My timeline consisted of a Ford Mustang, Turbo Diesel Volkswagen Jetta, a Mazda MX6, a Geo Prism, and a 325i BMW purchased on a whim instead of a Honda Accord.

After the Beamer repairs kept sabotaging my savings account, the practical side of me drove me back to the seat of a Honda Accord. By my mid 30's I was over just having a car for the sake of getting from point A to point B. Unknowingly, my burning desire for better caused me to practice visioning. I knew wanted to drive 'the car' of my dreams, so I began to play - imagine - 'see' myself in a Mercedes. It was easy, effortless and fun.

Whenever one cruised by me in passing I affirmed, "My soul says yes Lord!" It wasn't long before my riding down the street became akin to someone looking at a handful of M&Ms … hard and colorful on the outside, yet plain chocolaty on the inside. Let me explain. Although the outer appearance of my car clearly spelled Honda Accord, *in my mind* as I drove, it was a full-fledged Mercedes Benz. I 'saw' it and treated it as such … so it was in my world.

When my friends and I went out to eat, if valet service was available, you can best believe my '*Honda-Benz*' was going to be parked in style. Undoubtedly, by it being the only non-luxury car in the valet section every time, it stood out like a sore thumb amongst the real Benz, Bentleys, Masseratis, Lamborghinis and Porsches.

Ask me if I cared?

Several girlfriends would gingerly ask me, "*Girl why are you letting them valet your car?*" My reply was always the same – "*I'm practicing for my Benz, when I get it, it will be parked right there with the rest of them bad boys*!" Some laughed. A few said, "*Alright nah!*" Others looked at me funny. Who knows, they may have all secretly been embarrassed in the Valet line with me. Perhaps, they thought I was one of *the crazy ones*, at least until the actual manifestation.

While smack dab in the middle of my *'Honda-Benz'* days, a dear Sistah-friend of mine and I walked out of Pappasito's Cantina. Along the side of the building, my attention to what she was saying shifted. There, I spotted two gorgeous new Mercedes Benz parked one in front of the other. Coming to an abrupt stop, I grabbed her arm to get her attention and said, "Ooh wee girl, look!" My sudden excitement and movement visibly startled her. "That's going to be us one day, parked just like that." I zealously and prophetically continued. Having witnessed God perform many amazing miracles in my life, she didn't miss a beat before she agreed, "Yes indeed, Sister I 'see' us!"

That Benz vision agreement is something we still laugh about, reflect upon and draw strength from. When faced with obstacles today we are encouraged to keep trusting, believing and speaking in faith because what we saw/said many years ago did become our reality. Hers was gold, and mine was silver.

For the longest, we deliberately parked side-by-side or bumper-to-bumper wherever we went. Please don't take this example as materialistic or braggadocios because that is not my intent. I wholeheartedly realize that a car *is just* a car, but over past thirteen years, I've continued to proudly hand over my sho'nuff real Benz keys to valet attendants.

Now, a dream car may not be that big of a deal for you. Perhaps it's a home, business venture, mate, vacation destination, healing or dream job you've got tucked away in you heart of hearts. Whatever it is, know you too can have what you 'see'- say in faith. It's not luck it's blessed.

Does having a vision and speaking words that agree with that vision really produce like that? Yep, it sure does! Words have tremendous power. **Proverbs 8:21** - Life and death are in the power of your tongue, and *you will have what you say*. Believe and receive … don't doubt and do without **NOT 1 MORE DAY**.

If prior to this day you have spoken words contrary to what you 'see' and desire, please **STOP!** Stop right now. Do not speak against yourself, your abilities or your vision **NOT 1 MORE DAY.** Consider this very moment as your Divinely appointed time to grant yourself permission to **let** your words bring forth, produce, and manifest your heart's desires.

Romans 4:17 instructs us to speak those things that *be not* as though they were. ***Say it*** until it shows up. I'd imagine this verse provided the basis for the worldly "fake it 'til you make it" motto, but *this here right here* what I'm telling you *ain't* fake … it's God's word and His promises; *ain't* nothing fake about that!

"Have faith in the LORD your God and you will be upheld; have faith in his prophets and you will be successful." 2 Chronicles 20:20

You need healing? *Say, by His stripes <u>I AM</u> healed.* You need money? *Say, every one of my needs have already been met by Jehovah Jireh according to His riches in glory.* You want a mate? *Say, my perfect spouse is waiting to meet me and when God knows we are ready for each other, he/she will be presented.* You need a job? *Say, there is a position being created for me right now. Doors are opening in my favor and my gift has made room for me.* You have a loved one who has lost their way and needs deliverance? *Say, I 'see' ________ totally restored, set free and living well.* **Say it** as though it has already happened – **Speak it forward**.

Don't say what you see with your natural eyes … *say* what your spirit 'sees'. *Say* what you desire. Stop using the power of your spoken words to reinforce that which you don't want, aint right, is not happening. **Speak it forward**. Speak with expectancy. Watch intently as the words of your mouth, aligned with the desires of your heart and God's word begin to manifest those things you've spoken.

> **Say 2 Self:** The fruits of my lips will ripen in my life; My words determine the sweetness of my fruit!

(SSI) Self Soul Inventory:

1. What do you 'see' when you look in the mirror?

2. What image are you holding onto that is a disservice to your highest and grandest self?

3. What is your vision for the next 12 months of your life?

4. How do you intend to show up and be seen by others?

5. What will it take for you to 'see' yourself as God sees you?

<u>**Prayer 2 Pray Today:**</u>

Dear Heavenly Father,

*Help me to see myself as You see me. Help me to overlook my faults, my flaws and my shortcomings so that I can embrace the **TAGs** you've entrusted to me. Help me to be more positive, kind and loving towards myself in appreciation of who You have created me to be. Help me not look to others for validation or approval and teach me to search Your Holy Word for my security and identity.*

Thank You Father for giving me the authority to speak blessings, provision, deliverance, healing and peace into my life. Thank You for giving me the power to speak life and death to the problems, obstacles and difficult situations I face from day to day. Thank You Lord God for making me the head and NOT the tail, the lender and NOT the borrower and for keeping me above and NOT beneath my circumstances. Thank You for giving me the victory over sin, sickness, poverty and lack.

*Now Lord, please allow me to shine this little light of mine brightly and bring glory to Your name by letting others know of your goodness and mercy. Use me as you see fit for the building of Your Kingdom and liberation of Your children. Use my life as a witness and testimony of Your ability to do the impossible and abundantly bless those who dare to trust and believe in You. I decree and declare that I will begin speaking only what I desire to see from this day forward. **NOT 1 MORE DAY** will I allow the words of my mouth to create that which I do not want to manifest in my life. **NOT 1 MORE DAY** will I doubt Your ability to do exceedingly abundantly all that I can ask or think. Because I am who You say I am Lord, I know I can do whatever You say I can do in Jesus' mighty name I pray. Amen*

CHAPTER 9

When Silent Suffering Surfaces

"Everyone you meet is fighting a battle you know nothing about. Be kind. Always."

I know not one, single, solitary person who's never made a mistake - do you? Exactly! Mistakes are how we learn – when we know better, we can do better. In the field of education, educators are trained to create 'safe' learning environments for their students – a place where they can freely explore, express and evolve.

In creating this 'safe' zone, the ground rules are set and include: no name calling, no judging of others, no shaming and no rude comments. The same rules of safety hold true for a good counseling or coaching session. Yet, in way too many homes, this is far from the case – there are no such rules of conduct and much damage is done as a result.

Depending on the home you were raised in as a child, making a mistake was either viewed as the end of the world or the beginning of knowledge.

The End of the World: In this type of household mistakes are synonymous with criminal acts. The child's entire character is on trial and the punishment is severe for even the slightest mishap. Physical, emotional and mental wounds are inflicted here, and deep ugly scars remain for years to come. Indelible words of defeat, disdain and anger are hurled insensitively at the child's least shortcoming.

In fact, much of what is said and done by the parents to the children in this environment gets reenacted in their adult lives. Their parents treated them in this manner, and they end up repeating a painfully dysfunctional learned behavior (toxicity) which is now passed down for years and years to innocent generations. It's a pattern. A curse.

A vicious cycle of mis-*taken* identity spinning and creating emotional abuse develops, spanning years, even decades, spawning from unresolved anger, hurt and shame.

The blameless, severely mentally abused child grows up and later enters a relationship with another person who is highly likely to have experienced the same. Like attracts like. Darkness finds comfort in darkness and these dysfunctional interactions form their relationship's foundation.

Should this toxic affair end, both parties feel even more broken than before, further reinforcing harmful negative beliefs which were imparted in childhood. *My God!* As adults, these two damaged souls must now somehow work in pain, live in torment, function from a dark place and attempt to mainstream in society.

To survive, they assume a victim's mentality and like a broken record playing repeatedly, they believe no one loves them, they are unworthy of kind treatment, they must hurt others before they get hurt and that the world is a cold cruel place to be in. Hence, this fact: *hurt people, hurt people.*

With this faulty dog-eat-dog belief system, the very thing people need and crave more than life itself -LOVE- becomes an unrealistic, undesirable expectation and is considered a weak person's emotion. In their survival of the fittest mindset, strong people don't fall in love or show emotions. Consequently, they shut down. Walls are erected.

Sadly, the childlike innocence of millions of women and men alike has been snatched away in the coldness of a past void of emotion. Many living among us have been victimized as children by a family member who, out of their own dark empty places, used their young bodies as a source of inoculation against unresolved pain and disappointment. These victims subconsciously continue repeating this sick cycle by misconstruing sex for love, meeting and infecting others with a one-sided self-serving encounter. When looking for love in all the wrong places, sex often becomes the drug of choice.

It temporarily eases the pain of former rejection and mistreatment. It masks the pain and gives the illusion of a deeper human connection, but sadly, the *intercourse* between the two leaves even more scars when it fails to produce a viable relationship. It may sound like, look like and feel like the real thing until a child is conceived and later born, bringing the fantasy to a prematurely ejaculated reality.

Unfortunately, the birth of this tiny innocent soul carries with it the responsibility to solidify and satisfy something that had no substance from the start … it was simply a temporary fix for the pain. A fling. A hit. A brief season. A quick fix. Hence, without a wholesome relationship of mutual love, respect and commitment, the unborn child is often rejected at conception; incubated in a dejected womb. Unwelcomed. Unwanted.

Suddenly and abruptly, duty illuminates the ever-so passionate delusion. It wasn't love. It was merely a self-seeking, self-serving filler, an attempt to 'feel better.' Devastation creeps in as accusations and excuses form a gulf of hatred bridged by a constant need for formula and diapers.

All too often, the woman is left alone to raise this 'love seed.' Left to figure out what went wrong and how to make things right for the life she is now solely responsible for … she turns to another random male or perhaps even a female for validation, companionship and love. Unfortunately, he/she may also be broken and bruised from a too troubled past which causes him/her to view this bruised Diva as prey.

Tragically, her child or children are distortedly seen by this new partner as an extended love potion to anesthetize their own unresolved pain. Erred judgement and illness of mind disrupts, hijacking the innocence, scarring and marring the formerly unblemished young seedling(s).

Shattering identities and destroying any sense of security, the silent confusion and inexhaustible anger make it difficult for the child/children to freely enjoy child-like folly.

Walking around in shame caused by hidden acts of physical violation and uninvited exploitation, wondering what they did wrong to deserve such dark secretive consideration; they begin to act out – speak out – cry out, but no one is paying attention.

No one sees.

No one hears.

No one cares.

No one knows why.

Somehow the cycle has been repeated. Another generation violated, robbed and left to find the pieces of their shattered souls.

School suddenly becomes a battleground, a stage with an audience of adults who, if they are not careful, will misdiagnose the acting out – speaking out – crying out and push this broken-spirited child further away by labeling them...medicating them…denying them participation in the very social activities that are vital for their inner healing and self-acceptance.

Other students in the school, many victims themselves, are keen at sniffing out like-kind and to anesthetize their own unspoken pain, they end up bullying the already broken young seedling. Sadly, we hear far too many news stories and read newsfeed after newsfeed about those who took their own lives to escape the day-to-day taunting …

unable to survive the mean, harsh world around them,
unable to understand why, unable to speak up or speak out,
they give up. No one saw. No one heard. No one cared,
until it was too late.

Many of you know this story personally. Someone
holding this book right now has lived an invisible life
because of being "seen" too soon and has also longed to
break free from the memory, the pain, the silence, but
didn't know how. The enemy torments you day and night
about someone disclosing your truth, shaming you and
destroying the image you portray because of what
happened to you or what you may have experienced in the
past.

You live in fear of being called out for a crime you
didn't commit – for an abusive cycle in which you didn't
enroll – singled out for being a victim who had to either
retreat or retaliate to survive. This misery has caused you
to settle for less than you deserve in relationships and

makes you feel unclean, unworthy of real love, mutual respect and a good life. This dark secret has kept you from letting your light shine … has kept your head bowed.

Perhaps you've survived thus far by self-medicating with one or more worldly painkillers: alcohol, drugs, sex, material things, pornography, food etc., just to get through the day. But God says, "You don't have to suffer in silence or seclusion **NOT 1 More Day** … enough is enough!" He wants you to know that **He** sees you! **He** hears you! **He** cares, and it's NOT too late!

It's time for the truth to prevail … most everyone you have met, or will ever meet in this life, has gone through something debilitating and needs, or has needed, God's healing power to get free at some point. Hold your head up. Lift your eyes up.

I am extremely ecstatic, proud and thankful for my life-long friend, Nicole Scott, who recently published her story,

The Frog Chronicles: The Aftermath of Sustained Silence,
on behalf of those who have also shed silent tears. In it she
speaks up and speaks out for the little girl in her who had
no choice and no voice. In it she gives a transparent
account of how the painful aftermath spilled over into her
adult life and colored her relationships. With heartfelt
recollection and avid disclosure of every account, she sets
herself free. Nicole's healing is manifesting, and **NOT 1
More Day** will she be forced to suffer in silence alone.
Praise God!

Accept the good news today that you too can be healed
from your afflictions, healed to help others and healed to
live the abundant life God intended for you before you
were ever formed in your mother's womb. Healed without
scars. Healed to soar! **Psalm 107:20** says,
*"He sent His word, and healed them, and delivered them
from their destructions."* I'm reminded by that verse of a
poem I wrote in 1993 entitled **His Choice**:

Hidden in the darkness waiting for the light
A precious soul lies sheltered from a world that isn't right.
Echoes of hatred and fear penetrate the walls
It cries for a chance to live, but its cries are too small.
Surviving day by day on the Divine Master's grace
Wanting desperately to be mainstreamed into The Human Race.

Helplessly, yet hopefully, it strives to find rest
In the warmth of a womb that feels cursed and unblessed.
Hearing painful words of rejection, shame and disgust
From the very one God has chosen for it to love and trust.

Who can fight for this little soldier's life?
Who dares to contend with all the bickering and strife?
Who is bold enough to speak words of anti-choice?
Who is unafraid of being God's protective voice?
How can a mind that is thoroughly made up
Be changed from the destruction floating in death's bitter cup?

In the distant midnight hour God could hear an old saint say,
"Oh Lord have mercy and accept these words I pray.
Lord, you've got all power in your kind and gentle hands
And you control the destiny of every woman, child, and man.
So, Lord, I beseech you to step in right now
Save this little one from the jaws of abortion somehow.
Thank you, Lord, in advance for moving before the dawn of day
And stopping the 'procedure' that was scheduled for today.
I praise you Lord Jesus for hearing my humble plea
And for the host of angels standing guard around the uterine
sea."

Months later, in the coldness of a nearby delivery room
Lay another of God's creation who escaped the graven tomb.
A loud strong cry was yelled gladly for all to hear
Proving that miracles of God are real and do undoubtedly
appear.

Yes, now a little one had a chance to grow and spread His word
All because someone prayed that night, and its small faint cry
was heard!

©JJG1993

I decree and declare in the name of Jesus that any residual chains of bondage from childhood abuse and neglect are being broken even as you read. Healing is taking place in your spirit, in your mind and in your heart. Yes, finally someone understands how you feel. (((HUGS)))

God wants you to know today that your life matters. You are special in His sight. You are not alone. I love you, and God loves you. He knows you …

Jeremiah 1:5 (KJV) *"Before I formed thee in the womb, I knew thee; and before thou camest forth out of the womb I sanctified thee, and I ordained thee a prophet unto the nations."*
And guess what? Not only does He know you personally;

His mind is full of you (He is *mindful* of you).

> *"For I know the thoughts that I think toward you, saith the LORD, thoughts of peace, and not of evil, to give you an expected end."* **Jeremiah 29:11**

Say 2 Self: I trust God's plan for my life and give my pain to Him. It was not in vain and will bring healing to others.

Whatever evil doing happened to you as a child, as a teenager, while you were single, in your marriage, or after your divorce does not *define* you - it *refines* you! In fact, **Romans 8:28** lets us know that the God we serve specializes in taking what was meant for evil and making it work together for your good. Believe it or not, Beloved you are better because of what you've been through, so refuse to be bitter or feel battered. He didn't let it break you, but He will cause it to make you stronger, wiser and worthy of being used to help someone else. Your story is His glory! Trust the process and know that despite everything that could have or should have destroyed you, you are blessed! Know that the life you were living until now is NOT the expected end God has planned for you.

It ain't over.

This ain't it.

You ain't seen nothing yet!

If you don't believe me, check this out:

> *"But as it is written, eye hath not seen, nor ear heard, neither has it entered into the heart of man, the things which God hath prepared for them that love Him."*
> **1 Corinthians 2:9**

Your best is truly yet to come. Believe that! Receive that!

Say 2 Self: My best is yet to come. God has great plans for the rest of my life! Therefore, **NOT 1 More Day** will I walk with my head hung low, feeling bad or sad about the past … my worst days are behind me; my best days are ahead of me. I am His, and He is mine. My dark days are gone now, and I'm ready to shine!

Decide to take back your control - one day, one step, and one memory at a time! If you are sick and tired of being sick and tired today, here are 5 things you can do:

- ❖ **<u>Forgive</u>** and be willing let go of the painful past … you must forgive and release the person.

- ❖ **<u>Focus</u>** on the present – you are an adult now; you are in control, and you survived.

- ❖ **<u>Seek</u>** some type of spiritual or professional counseling from someone qualified to help you realize that none of what you experienced was your fault.

❖ **Pray** and ask God to heal the hurt. "He heals the brokenhearted and binds up their wounds." ~ **Psalm 147:3**

❖ **Decree and declare** - "This is the day that the Lord has made. I will rejoice and be glad. The transgressions of many generations before me, my parents and their parents do not belong to me and will not become mine. I refuse to allow the pain of my past to rob me, my children, my spouse or my future of **NOT 1 More Day.** It is now so, and it cannot be otherwise. I deserve to be loved, to be happy and to live an abundant life in Jesus' name. Amen"

(SSI) Soul Self-Inventory:

1. Which me do I 'see' when I look in the mirror? (Go deep)

2. What image are I holding onto that is a disservice to my highest and grandest self?

3. Am I 'seeing' myself *only* as I am and getting stuck where I am as a result?

4. How does the 'me' that I desire to be look? (Be very detailed)

5. What do I want to 'see' happening in my life consistently?

<u>My Prayer to Pray Today:</u>

Dear Heavenly Father, thank you for loving me enough to send these words to heal the parts of me that have been broken. Help me to forgive those who have trespassed against me. Help me to trust you to give them their just due because vengeance is yours, and your word promises that you will repay.

Help me to live the rest of my life with peace of mind, without anger or resentment, so I can live freely and abundantly; fulfilling my purpose as you intended. Thank you putting an end to my silent suffering and for setting me free by your word. Thank you for the plans you have for me that are good and not evil. Now Lord, I ask that you heal me completely from the inside out, so I can be used by you to heal others and bring glory to your name.

Protect my children and other little ones in every part of this world, Lord cover them with the blood of your Son Jesus Christ so that no weapon formed against them can prosper. Encamp mighty angels 'round about them to keep them pure and safe from all hurt harm and danger.

And please Lord God, convict all parents, relatives and others who have inflicted unnecessary physical, sexual and emotional pain upon your children; cause them to repent, recognize and cherish the gift of parenthood, a family and the very life they have been given ... make them better stewards of your children. Give them your patience, wisdom and understanding so that they can love like you love – unconditionally. Help us all work together to bring this generation up according to your perfect will.

In Jesus' mighty name I pray.
Amen.

CHAPTER 10

Your Life Matters … Choose You!

One of the greatest aspects of being a human being, alive on planet Earth, is our ability to choose. Many of us equate having choices with being in control. In fact, our survival instincts tell us that we'll survive if we have control, and this keeps us seeking control. This desire to obtain and maintain control keeps us on the hunt for the best choices. However, too many opportunities, too many options, too many opinions and too many vainly imagined obstacles make those choices difficult at times.

As a believer, I knew to seek God for wisdom, direction and His perfect plan, but somehow, I'd always get tangled up in listening to the opinions of others.

He'd speak, and they'd speak. In considering *this,* I'd also have to reconsider *that,* and the volley in my mind continued. Fear would grip me, and I'd end up either retracting from, or not acting at all on, the vision nudging me towards a different way of life. My vision wanted me free. I knew that the Spirit of the Lord was upon me **(Isaiah 61:1-7)** and that He had anointed me to do a great work for Him, but I just couldn't figure out how or where to start.

Well, I'm sure you can guess what happened … absolutely nothing! Despite the many amazingly inspiring books I'd read: *The Power of Positive Thinking, Charting Your Own Course, The Secret, The Purpose Driven Life and The Art of Self-Leadership*, just to name a few, I was paralyzed by a mediocre lifestyle, living paycheck to paycheck and perpetuating everyone else's dream.

On the surface, I had every outer marking and making of 'success' neatly outlined with a marginal degree of happiness.   However, I was never able to shake the cloak of doing something greater weighing heavily upon my shoulders or the recurring theme playing in my soul: *"There's gotta be more to life than this."*

I'd always known that I was an author, a poet, and an empowering speaker who desired to spend her years travelling, spreading God's word and helping others live a more fulfilling life. Continuously seeking to please the masses instead of pleasing the One who created me for His glory, I wandered on … pulled and stretched all over.

Not surprisingly, when I was laid off in 2006, my creative juices were free to flow, and my mind was full of zeal, determination and a clear sense of purpose. My entrepreneurial blood pumped furiously, and every endeavor of interest I pursued offered financial and time freedom in exchange for hitting the pavement with gusto. Breaking records was my goal. Making millions was the target.

However, on a part-time and more immediate income generating basis, I facilitated life skills sessions, provided vocational training and taught computer classes for some of the most enlightening audiences I had ever encountered. Fun-loving, multitalented men and women whom society stereotypically labeled *'at-risk adults'*.

Together we discussed the tough lessons life had taught, revisited dark places that pain protectively tucked away as I sought to awaken their hope and resurrect their long-lost dreams for a better tomorrow. Letting my 'light' shine daily, seeing lives changed, helping fixed mindsets shift and making a difference … I woke up early each morning driven by purpose fueled with focused energy. For the first time in my life, on the path to pursuing my dream – feeling connected to my God and humanity – for the first time in my life, I experienced living intentionally!

Like a cruel obnoxious master, a deep dark plaguing apprehension regarding my long-term financial wellbeing became more of a driving force than fulfilling my God-given assignment. Akin to the Apostle Peter when he was walking on the water, I began looking down. I began to sink into an underlying deep fear of being overcome by poverty even though I knew better. This kind of trickery is like a thief in the night that steals your identity, robs you of precious time, destroys your vision and kills your desire. With eyes no longer on my vision, focusing in fear on a future that I couldn't see … it wouldn't be long before I returned to the pseudo-safety of a 'regular' full-time job with 'benefits' and a 'steady' paycheck every two weeks.

In 2009, I acquiesced, breathed my last breath of purposefulness and made my final descent into the ferocious façade of a financial safety net. Somehow, to salvage my economic existence, I knowingly ignored the still small voice inside that kept beckoning me to activate my faith and press on in faith towards purpose. Overriding my vision and disconnecting from my path; joining thousands, possibly even millions, of others in this world who awake early and go to bed late - day after disappointing day- trading their purpose, passion, **TAGs** and time for pennies on the dollar just to make ends meet … I sold out. Although I knew better than to give in to the feverish **SDTs** (self-defeating thoughts) aka *stinkin-thinkin'* in my mind trying to convince me that God's ability to provide wasn't working; threatening that if I chose to continue working part-time in the area of my passion, living intentionally and waking up on purpose, I'd be broke and homeless … that's exactly what I did.

I gave in. I doubted.

Controlled and deeply oppressed by the fear of poverty, year after excruciating year, I dug my heels into the muck and the mire of institutionalized mediocrity. Continuing education credit upon credit, certification upon certification, I built my impressive professional portfolio. Striving to master the educator's dance, establish my astute worthiness in such a scholarly arena and rise to the esteemed ranks of admin life, I continued. Losing sight of my purpose, becoming enthralled with the ever-tallying report-card-like evaluating system, my insatiable determination to excel dominated. The obsession to achieve professional peer acceptance, recognition and respect prostituted me. There was no pleasure in my pursuits, no passion and no purpose other than to be acknowledged as one of them … to make my robustly creative mind fit into this claustrophobic coffin of rote processes and flat-lined procedures.

As promotions came, positions changed, and pressures increased – my passion and my purpose were progressively dying; unbeknownst to me at the time, so was

I. Obviously, in the eyes of many classroom teachers, friends, colleagues and especially my dear mother, when I signed up, showed up and soared up in the field - I had arrived.

In my own defeated darkened eyes, I couldn't have been more of a disappointment … a failure. Everything I'd encouraged my mislabeled 'at-risk' adult students to think and believe, I myself had gone against.

Who was this person I'd become?

I struggled to make sense of this 'good' life I'd worked so diligently to create. I ceased living what I preached. I exchanged making a difference for making a living. I questioned my own empowering, liberating, motivating and inspiring advice. I couldn't have been any farther from my true life's calling or from my true self.

Death of my purpose and self-inflicted destruction imminently encroached upon me. Day after draining day, I plodded along smiling on the outside while angry on the inside about becoming such a sellout and a cheap one at that. Misery, anxiety and depression gently snuck upon me like a slow looming fog.

My entire body ached in the mornings when I arose. Tirelessly, I wrestled against my own desires to be a light, a source of hope and inspiration - deliberately repressing them - to make myself function - to navigate through the day. Despite the painful resistance of knees that locked, cracked and popped as I forcibly demanded they walk-the-walk, I shuffled on.

Much like a freshly fallen pecan lodged inside of a shiny silver nutcracker squeezed into distinct halves, my lower back ached relentlessly with each dutiful step. Struggling every working hour against myself, despite my ever-aching body, my numbed passion, my splintered soul and my dimmed light ... I pressed on. Each day became more mentally, physically, emotionally and spiritually exhausting than the one before.   Stubbornly, I battled within, tirelessly and hopelessly, attempting to conform to the predictable routines of an inexorably rigid and regulated venue.

It wasn't long before the pull and tug of my purpose wouldn't let me sleep at night, regardless of how fatigued and drained I may have been from my laborious day's journey. Late in the midnight to wee morning hours I tossed and turned, trying to remain asleep, as thoughts of what my life could be tantalized, swirled and scrolled swiftly in my head.

Anxiously, I lived for Fridays and was repulsed by Sundays because they signified the beginning and the ending of my respite from the prestigious prison, I'd contracted myself into. Many were my emotional wounds as the warfare kept raging and wreaking havoc on my captive soul. Like a dripping water faucet, echoing in my tormented mind were the words my mother would use to jokingly, yet prophetically, remind me from time to time, *"The world is waiting on you!"* She was right, and with the blatant reality of more years behind me than I had remaining, I knew I had to alter my course.

There were so many books still incubating in my spirit from decades of restrained imagination and repressed inspiration. So many lost, lonely and longing souls, wailing and waiting on a word of hope to set them free – my distractions kept them there. So many people I encountered who, like me, were living beneath their **TAGs** and God-intended potential. So much work, yet so little time. The vicious cycle of inner and outer torment continued. Brutal was the combat of conformity, duty and social acceptance.

Not realizing then what I realize now: job dissatisfaction is the number one risk factor contributing to suffering a fatal first heart-attack. Undoubtedly, yet unknowingly, the campaign for my premature death was well underway. In fact, not only was I at an imminent risk of physically dying; my soul had already died. My heart had long stopped beating. I had no pulse left to pursue what I believed in. I was walking, talking, smiling and living … dead. Dead to my passion and purpose. Dead to my true self. Gone!

Seemingly on cue, God allowed my mind, body and spirit to collaboratively combust, sending an irrefutable message which had I not heeded, was sure to deliver me an untimely sunset. A life-threatening wake-up call forced me to abruptly disconnect from the self-styled safe script I had auditioned for and society so munificently casted me to perform.

A physician's diagnosis revealed a jolting 195/110 blood pressure reading, a body weight so grand that the scale couldn't register my heft, news of my body being riddled with chronic pain, inflammation and in adrenal fatigue. Further evaluation discovered that I was mentally and emotionally tapped out – on the brink of a mental power outage. That initial medical prognosis teetered and tottered upon my admission into a 'psych' hospital, pending my willingness to release whatever had me in this condition.

So, I stopped fighting knowing that I had to let go of this state of mere existence I'd created. Honestly, it took a jeopardous toll on my life for me to choose me, truly acknowledge my purpose and accept its invitation.

Realizing I couldn't afford to trudge **NOT 1 MORE DAY** down this deathly desolate path, regardless of the uncounted future costs, I said yes! Yes, to life, to my God and to my light. Boldly and thankfully, I resolved, "I'm done. I must be done. I will surely die if I keep putting myself through this agony – I want to live. I want to be free. I want to be healed." Looking up, and crying out to God from my rock's bottom, I became motionless. Silent.

I ceased and desisted. My choice to live and not die in the role I'd forced myself to play was evident. I heeded the warning … I surrendered. Upon finally succumbing to that still small voice inside of me, I deliberately exhaled.

My induced silence and humbled stillness facilitated my acceptance of the harsh reality: I had been afraid to trust Him totally with my life, my finances and my future. Ashamed, frazzled and frayed, I wept.

Blurredly gazing through my tears at the fear which had stealthily gotten the best of me, rendering me mentally and physically helpless … too afraid to believe in my **TAGs** ability to change my own life, I apologized profusely to my God. At that moment, I vowed to waste

NOT 1 MORE DAY pursuing anything other than His

perfect plan. Alas! The mask I'd worn for so long lifted.

Choosing to seek His face, pursue His will, and let

my light shine was easy. No matter the price my pride had

to pay, I committed to living intentionally, fully by faith,

and unapologetically guided by my passion fueled purpose.

The moment I vehemently arose to my own rescue

and agreed to set myself free from the crippling bondage

fear had fashioned ... I was revived. Reconnecting to God's

plan, instead of the one I chose out of fear and conformity,

resurrected me, and over the next eight months, He gently

breathed invigorating life back into my formerly *de-ceased*

state.

Ever so lovingly, my Creator, the One who called

me as a child and patiently waited for me to acknowledge

His will -my purpose – granted me much needed peace and

relaxation. Without resisting, I allowed myself to breathe again -to dream again - to choose life … to choose me.

My time had indeed come. Still, I would have to make the final decision to officially part ways and sever ties with my pseudo-safety net … diving head-first into my appointed anointed *'Life-light Work,'* with no holds barred.

That was the difficult part, a huge test of my faith marking the unveiling of a brand-new purpose filled journey towards financial independence and self-employment.   Although much relieved and reassured that this newfound freedom and dependence on God was the right decision, somehow, I struggled within. Charting a new course, letting go of the status quo, ditching my employee mindset, foregoing a decent paycheck every two weeks, and departing from that seemingly solid foundation despite the discontent it produced was a huge step.

No doubt … shifting would take time. Unexpectedly, deep within the throws of an extreme transitioning process, my purpose and passion for coaching and empowering others was confirmed. Purpose founded and grounded me. By Divine design, a former colleague called for advice concerning a wearisome professional predicament.

Now this wasn't just some random caller who may have heard of my life-coaching ability; someone who knew of my **TAGs** or perhaps had been referred to me, this was a special person God used miraculously many years prior to guide me in the early stages of a newly acquired career. His vast content knowledge, remarkably consistent professionalism, respectful leadership and admirable character, in my aspiring eyes, were impeccable.

As a mentor, he never failed to provide the type of nurturing advice a father would give to his offspring as he prepared them for success in life. No question of mine was ever too shallow; never was there a moment when I required guidance that he deemed himself too busy to give his full attention. My efforts to implement his strategies and suggestions no matter how large or small, were always applauded in joyful support.

Many, many moons later, the law of sowing and reaping came into full effect concerning our relationship. Noticing the Caller ID flashing upon my phone screen one festive Sunday afternoon, I knew something had to be amiss. Chatting on the phone simply was not a routine we'd ever shared. In fact, I can't recall him ever phoning me prior to that day.

Instantly, at the sound of his voice, the Spirit in me quickened, and I sensed a quandary of sorts in the making. Doubt, fear, desolation and defeat were rampant in his tone.

In empathetic desperation, I searched within the chambers of my heart and soul to bring him peace and calm. Like a busted and gushing water main, he recounted instance after instance of workplace bullying. Clearly an attack of the enemy tormented him to the point of crying out for a listening ear and a word of comforting direction.

Never in my wildest dreams could I have imagined him needing me for anything, especially advice about his life. He exemplified such strength and wisdom. But God! Honored and more than eager to help, I pushed past the fury laden adrenaline flooding my veins from the insane list of workplace attacks he'd been the target of. Together, we began plowing through the madness behind the countless contrived infractions, subtle sabotages and character assassinations he had painfully summoned up.

My heart ached for him as I fought hard to provide clear, unbiased interpretations, wise counsel and viable solutions. How could anyone in their right mind be so callous and cruel to a gentleman of his demeanor? It disturbed me greatly when I sensed my former mentor struggling to hold back tears as painful stories continued to pour from his wounded soul. Sadly, yet honorably, he was determined to hang in there and finish strong until the end of the fiscal year despite his vastly weakened state.

However, his delicateness of mind and stress-ladened existence dictated otherwise. I advised him to seriously consider stepping down from the vicious rollercoaster ride and pause for his own cause. I emphatically told him that his time had come to put his own best interest first.

"There comes a time in every person's life when you have to deliberately choose to do what's best for you and yours. Especially if you have a sincere desire to do the right thing even in the 'wrongest' of circumstances." **Jacq Green**

This meant work: obtaining a medical evaluation, availing himself to my continued coaching and willingly making a transition to the other side of this inopportune madness. Reluctantly, he contemplated the validity of my 'drastic advice' and the severity of the toll his workplace drama created. Sensing his hesitation and discomfort, I gently reminded him of the instruction travelers are given prior to takeoff aboard an aircraft:

*"Passengers, please secure your seatbelts and make note of the oxygen masks hanging overhead. In the event of a loss in cabin pressure the mask will drop down. Those traveling with small children, please **secure your mask first** then proceed to place the child's mask on."*

He chuckled and affirmed hearing that before also. *"The cabin is losing pressure, your mask has dropped down ... right now, if you want to live you must put it on,"* I *calmly stated.* "You can't afford to let **NOT 1 MORE DAY** of that stress torment you, and the good news is you don't have to.

I further explained to him how he was expending an enormous amount of energy surviving while smiling through a deflated and demoted disposition, which was inevitably destroying his mind, body and spirit silently like an undetected termite infestation. Admittedly, he had spent numerous sleepless nights lying awake rehearsing the shrewd underhandedness of the day; dreading the dawning of another brutally vulnerable eight-hour boxing match.

His body tried to signal him of the damage when his hair began to thin, he broke out in unexplainable rashes and often felt his mental focus shifting and drifting, without permission, smack dab in the middle of a task, but these signs were ignored.

Guaranteeing him that if this work situation was sucking the very life out of him day after day, he could best bet his last dollar that his wife and children suffered too. Understanding the fragility of the male ego and the pressure he faced as the head of his household, I lovingly reassured him that these happenings were big bold capital letters written in neon ink upon the walls of his soul … warning of impending destruction along the path. This was bigger than masculinity, larger than any amount of perceived embarrassment he felt. This was his life, and only HE could stop the progression of his demise.

Clearly, a choice had to be made. Would he continue spiraling into oblivion for the sake of others or dare pull the plug on the enemy's plan by breaking the chains of bondage and seeking the help he needed? The guilt and shame of putting his personal, emotional and mental well-being in front of his career made his self-rescue difficult. As obvious as the answer may have been … his decision wasn't easy. Afterall, he didn't know what his next professional move would be. He feared a bad referral from his boss if he heeded my advice and left. His family was dependent upon his financial contributions to the household, and he wasn't a quitter. He wanted to finish the year even at to his own detriment. Major life decisions like the one he contemplated are never easy at first, but once you realize that life is all about choices and making the wrong ones for the right reasons could cost you the very air you breathe – the deal gets done. We talked. We prayed. We met face-to-face.

I encouraged and persuaded him to let go and trust God. Still sensing his reluctance, I prayed for the right words. God told me to ask him this, *"If you were your son, what advice would you give him?"* Without blinking an eye, he answered, *"I would tell him to leave."* When I told him to listen to what he just said, his whole demeanor changed.

Empathetically, and sympathetically, I shared with him my awakening and personal **NOT 1 MORE DAY** choice. We talked more. We prayed. We met again.

Together we worked through his complete transition and deliverance from cruelty. We thanked God in advance for taking what was meant for evil and turning it around for the good. He too made the decision, to live and not die **NOT 1**

MORE DAY in that position. He vehemently rose up to save himself and discontinued his daily subjection to harsh and hostile treatment. He came to his own rescue!

Armed with a prayed-up, made-up mind, a fresh resume in hand and a couple of peaceful night's sleep in tow, he shook off the cloak of defeat and presented his best self to the world. His restored faith, laser focus and renewed attitude were in full force.

Well, I'm proud to boastfully glorify the Lord by informing you of what happened shortly thereafter. God didn't tarry to present him with an offer he would have never received had he remained in his former state of fear- induced complacency.   My former mentor's breakthru, now one of my many coaching client success stories, resulted a promotion to another business sector where his **TAGs** and professional legacy were welcomed, appreciated and needed greatly. You see, God had already gone before him

to open the next door. Remember that He is no respecter of

persons – He can and will do the same for you.

> *"Lift not up your horn on high: speak not with a stiff neck. [6]For promotion cometh neither from the east, nor from the west, nor from the south. [7]But God is the judge: he putteth down one, and setteth up another."* **Psalm 75:6**

Say 2 Self: When I trust God and move in faith, great things happen for me. My next promotion is in His hands!

His best provision for my maltreated friend was

being created behind the scenes patiently awaiting an

opportunity to Divinely show up. All it took was a gentle

shift, an awakening, an earnest desire to live and not die; a

NOT 1 MORE DAY decision to put his oxygen mask on

first and trust God to supply the air, the energy and the

resources for his new journey.

Can you say increase, favor and provision? Yes, once again … My God came through! The fantastic news for you is that you too can be victorious instead of a hopeless victim in any area of your life. Your freedom, deliverance, breakthrough and blessings are just a prayer and decision away. You don't have to work or live under stress n' duress **NOT 1 MORE DAY** in Jesus' name.

While my faith was ignited, and I was beyond thrilled about what God had done for him, at that time my own shifting process was still incomplete. Having to progress onwards along my purposeful mission, an unsettling feeling continued to hover over me.

In fact, even after almost a year had passed, the new journey I'd embarked upon still required a tremendous amount of mental focus, physical rest, reflection and mental reprogramming. I had to stay closely connected to God and hold fast to His word, His purpose and a knowing deep on the inside that I was still headed in the right direction.

> "The entrance of thy words giveth light; it giveth understanding unto the simple. I opened my mouth and panted: for I longed for thy commandments. Look thou upon me, and be merciful unto me, as thou used to do unto those that love thy name. Order my steps in thy word: and let not any iniquity have dominion over me. Deliver me from the oppression of man: so, will I keep thy precepts. Make thy face to shine upon thy servant; and teach me thy statutes." **Psalm 119:133 KJV**

Say 2 Self: My shift, elevation and breakthrough to the next level demands clarity. I must stop, look and listen for God's instructions lest I fail/falter.

There were many good days and restful nights when I kept my eyes on His promise to supply my needs according to His riches in glory. On the contrary, my flesh would awake early to the entertainment of uninvited doubts and fears looming through the blinds as the sunlight beckoned me to another day. It was on those days that my faith had to be rekindled by God's still small voice, a song of praise, or a quick revisiting of my journal for a glance at how far I'd come.   Oftentimes a gentle reminder from within my core-about God's calling on my life provided the perfect fix.

Thoughts filled with images of thousands of hurting people in need of the 'Life-light Work' I was born to do kept my faith alive.   As weeks passed, with no clear path or plan of action in sight, I battled to remain free of the opinions of others regarding my impending shifted focus. My bank account balance voiced threats of complete financial ruin. The possibility of failing and facing social embarrassment loomed over me in relentless torment.

My fight to keep the faith in the face of too much reality almost wore me down. The battle cries waging war on my peace of mind went something like this … *"Quit being foolish. You're 52 years old, not twenty-two you know how irresponsible and unwise what you did is? Folks are retiring at your age and here you are thinking God has another plan and purpose for you. Plus, you know husband ain't feeling busta-faith-move you made and is not supporting you in this craziness. It's simple, all you gotta do is go back to work full-time like everybody else. What makes you think that you are so special that you don't have to have a 9-5? Girl please, you 'best-tah' stop tripping."*

Stuck between the familiarity of stale albeit stable employment and the intoxicating freedom of purpose-filled work and entrepreneurship, I sat. I couldn't confidently move forward, but at the same time I didn't want to go backwards. My **SDTs** (self-defeating thoughts) in cahoots with **RAL** (reason and logic) were running rampant causing me to deeply reconsider 'my' plight.

Drifting and shifting my eyes from God's promises, I felt myself sink just like Peter:

*When the disciples saw Him walking on the sea, they were terrified. "It's a ghost!" they said and cried out in fear. But Jesus immediately spoke up: **"Take courage! It is I. Do not be afraid."** "Lord, if it is You," Peter replied, "command me to come to You on the water." "**Come** hither," said Jesus. **Then Peter got down out of the boat, walked on the water, and came toward Jesus.** But when he saw the strength of the wind, he was afraid, and beginning to sink, cried out, "Lord, save me!" Immediately Jesus reached out His hand and took hold of Peter. **"You of little faith,"** He said, **"why did you doubt?"*** **Mark 26-31**

Realizing that I desperately needed to focus in faith, if I was to survive and thrive in this testing season, I went to battle aligning my words with the Word of God. By creating within me an arsenal of spiritual weapons to quench the negative images of defeat dancing in my mind as I attempted to fall asleep, I pressed on. But the doubtful questions persisted endlessly, OMG …

Was I doing the right thing?

Was I making the right decision?

Was this truly God's will for me?

Did I have what it takes to succeed?

At 52, I knew full well that a miscalculation at this point could prove disastrous. Through it all, my calling and purpose remained at the forefront of my reasonable, yet ungodly unfounded, fears. The struggle was real. The tug of war was brutal. My spirit and my flesh wrestled at odds.

I prayed. I fasted. I sang. I cried. Waves of anxiety washed up on the shores of my faith unexpectedly. My spirit would whisper, *"Be anxious for nothing Jacq. Remember to..."*

> *"Trust in the Lord with all your heart and lean not unto your own understanding. In all your ways acknowledge Him, and He will direct your path."* **Proverbs 3:5**

There were periods of deliberate isolation where I had to *be still and know*. I needed confirmation that I was moving according to God's perfect plan for my life. I had to hear it from Him. I had to be sure. I had to.

Relief and calm came as I felt God upholding me by His word; bracing my mind against the vicious currents of the unfamiliar territory I was treading.

Although on the surface I wavered and wondered in my thinking about returning to my pseudo-safety zone, at the core of my being, I knew my life's purpose couldn't simply

keep being tucked away. The pull and tug of my calling
was too strong. It wasn't letting go and neither could I.

Whenever I felt my resolve weakening, God stepped in. He sent me signs to confirm that what I was doing was exactly in agreement with His plans. People I hadn't seen, spoken to or even thought about in eons, I mean like ten, fifteen and twenty years respectively, started popping up in my life. Some appeared in person at random places, others reconnected on social media and a few surfaced via mutual friendships. People who were living the life my purpose and passion promised me. I witnessed them walking successfully on the very entrepreneurial waters that the enemy showed me were too deep for me to tread.

As days, weeks and months went by God continued to speak to me through their lives and their 'Light Work.' Much like actors/actresses entering and exiting stage on cue, they showed up, conveyed their messages and enlightened my soul. He sent a series of undeniably Divine encounters, imparting revelation upon revelation, and providing validation after validation to steady me.

Euphoria and confidence lifted my spirit allowing me to regain focus without fear; my vision solidified. Suddenly everything made sense! The enemy wanted me to shrink back, bow down and put a muzzle on my **TAGs** and calling.

He wanted me confined, bound and chained to job, living paycheck to paycheck, far away from those needing my light. He needed me hidden in the darkness of dutiful distractions and worldly busyness … where my voice would be silenced.

Instead of soaring freely coaching, writing, speaking and setting God's children free, I too would be living in bondage and this message of hope, inspiration and faith wouldn't have made it to the masses. *That's why he* kept trying to focus my attention on all that could go wrong, all that would be lost and all that I was risking by stepping out of my sinking boat. *That's why* he brutally persisted in his tactics to convince me that at this stage of my life, a solid source of income and tangible retirement plan was essential to my financial wellbeing. *That's why* he kept heckling and hissing in my mind that to depend on my gifts or my ministry to sustain me would prove foolish.

Say 2 Self: Whatever the enemy tells me is a lie and an attempt to deceive me into doubting God's power & ability.

Everything in the Word of God kept assuring me that He was my Provider, He loved me, He had great plans for my life and that He would supply every single one of my needs according to His riches in glory.

What a relief to know that my success, survival and total wellbeing was His responsibility NOT mine. Halleluiah, thank you Jesus!! All He required of me was trust in His promises. My childlike faith in His word to do what He said He would do was my ticket to peace, joy, abundance and real financial freedom. *"Just trust God Jacq. You know He's worthy ... trust Him. He's got you. You gotta believe that."* I reminded myself.

Sure enough, His history was solid with me. Indeed, I'd experienced His provision firsthand twelve years prior when I was laid off in 2006. With an ever-present memory of the victorious comeback He provided me in that season, I knew He'd prepared well me for this present moment.

Say 2 Self: When God wants me to master a lesson, He will allow the same material (situation/problem) to present itself many times – over and over again.

Fact is that leaning and depending on Him takes practice. Learning to become childlike in our trust and faith requires multiple applications ESPECIALLY with health/finances.

I knew it was time for me to exercise trusting Him with my financial wellbeing again. But was I up for the challenge? Honestly, I didn't want to be. *I wanted* to know the details, *I wanted* to be in control. *I wanted* to have a plan of action and see the finish line for myself. *I wanted* to be a big girl. My flesh kept resisting what my spirit needed to grow and go to the next level of faith.

Realistically, how could I not *want* to trust Him after all He'd proven to me? I fought to keep the faith and to trust His word. I wrestled with my independence and desire for financial security. I reminded myself that He *is* Jehovah Jireh – my provider. He hasn't stopped. He doesn't change. He *is* the same God today, yesterday and forever, so if He came through before, He would make a way … He'd come through. I knew this, I just had to believe it.

Clearly a faith-testing juncture awaited my decision. When that reality hit me, I knew I was back on the right track and that my faith was the vehicle required to transport me into a life of purpose. With knees shaking, palms sweating and eyes looking unto the hills from whence cometh my help, I drove over one hundred and eighty miles to hand deliver my resignation.

This scripture kept repeating in my head:

> *"And when he saw them, he said unto them, Go shew yourselves unto the priests. And it came to pass, that, as they went, they were cleansed."* **Luke 17:14**

My **NOT 1 MORE DAY** mindset and lifestyle was solidified at that defining moment, thus becoming my new reality. From that pivotal day until this one, I've not once regretted my decision to choose to live on purpose, walk by faith and trust God. My faith has grown by leaps and bounds as He's provided beyond my wildest imagination.

I've traveled more, stressed less and can honestly report to you that I'm living my very best life right now. It has been, and continues to be, an *awe-mazing* journey!

Won't you join me?

Be determined to walk by faith. Dare to trust God for what you need and want. Seek His word for assurance and live. Eliminate fearing the one decision capable of unlocking your blessings and changing not only your destiny, but also the future of others! Someone somewhere is waiting and depending on you to lead the way.

Your best life is waiting on you. You must break free!

In the words of Steve Harvey, *"Jump!"*

By now, you probably have an idea or two about an area you would like to change in your life (physically, financially, relationally, spiritually, socially, professionally, etc.), lasting change requires faith in God, confidence in yourself and a burning desire to make a difference. The mere fact you desire change is a sure indication that God is nudging you to make it happen. **Psalm 37:4** says that ***"If you delight yourself in the Lord, He will give you the desires of your heart."***

When your desire aligns with His plan for your life, the sky is no limit for what you can and will accomplish.

Don't be content to sail in the sea of mediocrity **NOT 1 MORE DAY**. Step out of the boat of simple existence and choose to start living your best life now!

"Go get your blessings ... it's your time!" - **Mary Mary**

(SSI) Soul Self-Inventory:

1. What will it take for you to trust God with your life? Your dreams? Your finances?

2. What will it cost you (mentally, to keep living just as you are right now?

3. How many people are depending on you to bust a faith-move?

4. How long will you remain in the pseudo-safety zone you have created?

5. When will you allow faith in God to rescue you from the bondage you are in?

My Prayer 2 Pray Today:

Heavenly Father,

*I thank you for renewing my body, my mind and my spirit with the powerful truth of your word. Please forgive me for the times I've listened to others instead of waiting to hear from you. Forgive me for not obeying your word or pleasing you with my faith. Forgive me for not using my **TAGs** and for settling for less than your best for me because I was playing it safe. Forgive me Lord God for instinctively succumbing to my* *fears instead of stretching out in obedience to your will. Forgive me for not trusting you with every aspect of my life and for unknowingly delaying the plans you have for me.*

Help me Lord God to wake up, rise-up and speak up now before it's too late. Help me to walk by faith not by sight; leaning and depending on you. Help me to know, understand and acknowledge my purpose. Give me the courage to trust myself, trust you, to overcome the opinions of others and to hold fast to what you have told/shown me. Lead me to the right people, send me to the right places and grant me enough wisdom, knowledge and understanding to use my light and let it shine to bring you glory.

In Jesus' name I decree and declare that the good work you have begun in me will be performed and that the purpose you had planned for me when you formed me in my mother's womb will be fulfilled. I will fight the good fight of faith – I will finish my life's course strongly, as I invite you to continue using my light to draw others to you.

Thank you for having mercy upon me and allowing me another chance to get it right. Thank you for your guidance, your promises and your love towards me. Thank you for the favor you send before me wherever I go and for new doors of opportunity awaiting me. In Jesus' name I pray.

Amen.

<u>Final Words</u>

Thank you for purchasing **NOT 1 MORE DAY!**

Nothing would make me happier than to hear from you about how something within these pages brought healing, hope and encouragement to your soul. If you would like for me to pray with you, speak to your church group or organization, contact me today! I'm here to serve.

Email: Mizjaq@HTM3Solutions.com

Facebook: HTM3 Solutions

To schedule individualized coaching or vision board workshops please visit www.htm3solutions.com or phone me directly @ 1.832.706.2200

Be blessed and remember:

You've got this because God's got you!

All the best,

Jacq (Mizjaq) Green

Made in the USA
Columbia, SC
02 August 2019